THE ULTIMATE
PETER RABBIT™

A VISUAL GUIDE TO THE
WORLD OF BEATRIX POTTER™

LONDON, NEW YORK,
MELBOURNE, MUNICH, AND DELHI

Senior Editor Camilla Hallinan
Senior Designer Anne Sharples
Designer Ellie Healey
Photographer Trish Gant
Picture Researcher Sean Hunter
Publishing Manager Cynthia O'Neill
Art Director Cathy Tincknell
Production Nicola Torode
DTP Designer Jill Bunyan
American Ediotor Margaret Parrish

First Published in the United States in 2002
by DK Publishing,
375 Hudson Street,
New York, New York 10014

06 07 08 09 10 9 8 7 6 5 4 3 2
KU011 – 11/06

DK books are available at special discounts when purchased in bulk for
sales promotions, premiums, fundraising, or educational use. For details, contact:
DK Publishing Special Markets
375 Hudson Street
New York, New York 10014
SpecialSales@dk.com

Library of Congress Cataloging-in-Publication Data

The Ultimate Peter Rabbit: a visual guide to the world of Beatrix Potter – 1st American ed.
p.cm.
Summary: Presents the life and work of Beatrix Potter through drawings, photographs,
letters, journal entries, excerpts, and more.
ISBN-10: 0-7894-8538-9
ISBN-13: 978-0-7894-8538-0
1. Potter, Beatrix, 1866-1943–Juvenile literature. 2. Potter, Beatrix,
1866-1943–Characters–Peter Rabbit–Juvenile literature. 3. Children's stories,
English–History and criticism–Juvenile literature. 4. Authors, English–20th
century–Biography–Juvenile literature. 5. Artists–Great Britain–Biography–Juvenile
literature. 6. Peter Rabbit (Fictitious character)–Juvenile literature. 7. Animals in
literature–Juvenile literature. 8. Animals in art–Juvenile literature. [1. Potter, Beatrix,
1866-1943. 2. Potter, Beatrix, 1866-1943–Characters. 3. Authors, English. 4.
Women–Biography.]

PR6031.072 Z89 2002
823'.912–dc21
[B]

Color reproduction by Media Development and Printing Ltd., UK
Printed and bound by Lake Book Manufacturing, Inc., USA

visit Peter Rabbit online at **www.peterrabbit.com**

Discover more at
www.dk.com

THE ULTIMATE PETER RABBIT

A VISUAL GUIDE TO THE WORLD OF BEATRIX POTTER ™

CAMILLA HALLINAN

Contents

"My dear Noel, I don't know what to write
to you, so I shall tell you a story about four
little rabbits whose names were Flopsy,
Mopsy, Cotton-tail and Peter."

LETTER TO NOEL MOORE,
SEPTEMBER 4, 1893

"It is much more satisfactory to address a real live child; I often think that that was the secret of the success of Peter Rabbit, it was written to a child – not made to order."

LETTER TO MRS. FRUING WARNE,
SEPTEMBER 26, 1905

MEET PETER RABBIT

IN 1893, A YOUNG WOMAN with a talent for storytelling wrote a letter about a naughty rabbit and sent it to a child she knew. Her story later became a little book, *The Tale of Peter Rabbit*. It was an instant and lasting success.

HELLO, PETER RABBIT

OVER 100 YEARS AGO Beatrix Potter created the tale of Peter, the naughty rabbit who disobeys his mother and goes on an adventure in Mr. McGregor's garden. It was her first book, and she wasn't confident about its prospects. "I am aware these little books don't last long even if they are a success," she said to her publisher. But she needn't have worried...

BEATRIX POTTER ILLUSTRATION OF PETER IN HIS FAMOUS BLUE JACKET

"Now run along and don't get into mischief," says Mrs. Rabbit. But Peter runs straight to Mr. McGregor's garden and squeezes under the gate!

CERAMIC FIGURINE OF MRS. RABBIT AND PETER

A CLASSIC

The Tale of Peter Rabbit has been in print since 1902, and translated into over 30 languages. Peter's image appears on everything from baby clothes and china to watering cans and wallpaper. He is one of the best-known children's characters in the world.

CHINA PLATE WITH PETER SQUEEZING UNDER THE GATE AND INDULGING IN FRENCH BEANS AND RADISHES

CUP AND SAUCER

AND t Peter, window, up The window Mr. McGre tired of runni went back to his

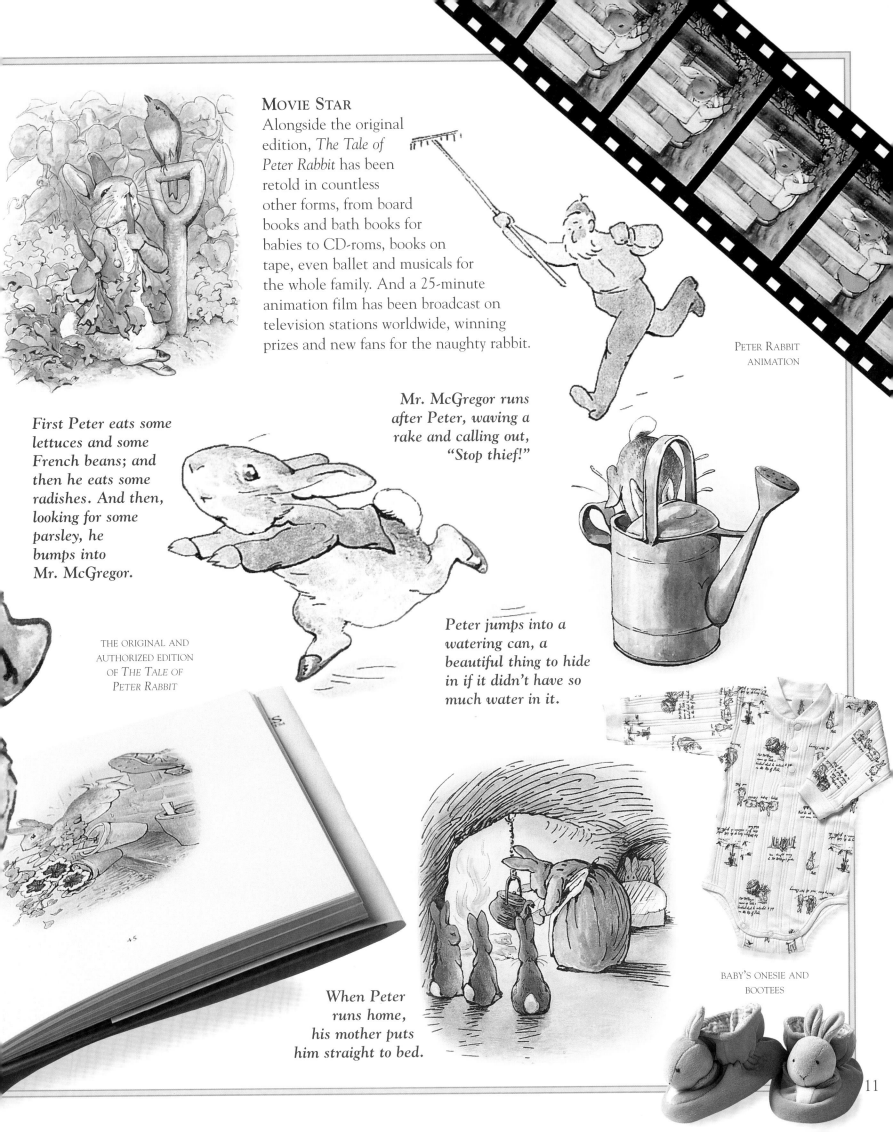

MOVIE STAR

Alongside the original edition, *The Tale of Peter Rabbit* has been retold in countless other forms, from board books and bath books for babies to CD-roms, books on tape, even ballet and musicals for the whole family. And a 25-minute animation film has been broadcast on television stations worldwide, winning prizes and new fans for the naughty rabbit.

PETER RABBIT ANIMATION

First Peter eats some lettuces and some French beans; and then he eats some radishes. And then, looking for some parsley, he bumps into Mr. McGregor.

Mr. McGregor runs after Peter, waving a rake and calling out, "Stop thief!"

THE ORIGINAL AND AUTHORIZED EDITION OF *THE TALE OF PETER RABBIT*

Peter jumps into a watering can, a beautiful thing to hide in if it didn't have so much water in it.

When Peter runs home, his mother puts him straight to bed.

BABY'S ONESIE AND BOOTEES

11

HOW IT ALL BEGAN

BEATRIX POTTER
AGED NINE,
PHOTOGRAPHED
BY HER FATHER

HELEN BEATRIX POTTER was born on July 28, 1866. The Potters lived in a large house on an elegant London square. Like all well-off families at the time, they had a full staff of servants. Beatrix was brought up by a nanny and saw far less of her parents than children do today. She and her brother spent most of their time in the schoolroom on the third floor of the house.

Beatrix was born in the reign of Queen Victoria. Her Majesty had nine children – seven appear in this portrait from 1864. Family life at the palace seems to have been more openly affectionate than it was for Beatrix and her brother Bertram.

PLAQUE ON THE SITE OF BEATRIX POTTER'S LONDON HOME

A LIFE OF LEISURE

When they married, Beatrix Potter's parents, Rupert Potter and Helen Leech, each had a sizeable fortune from the cotton trade in the north of England. He was a lawyer but preferred to discuss politics at his club or visit art galleries. She ran the house, called on friends, and arranged dinner parties.

Bolton Gardens (above), photographed by Beatrix Potter's father in 1889. The Potters' house at No. 2 Bolton Gardens was destroyed by a bomb in 1940.

UPSTAIRS DOWNSTAIRS

Life at Bolton Gardens required an army of servants. Coachmen and grooms looked after the Potters' carriages and horses at stables nearby. A housekeeper managed the domestic servants who kept the rooms spotless. A lady's maid assisted Helen Potter with dressing and letters. A butler announced visitors and oversaw the kitchen and dining room. And a nurse or nanny cared for the children.

BEATRIX HOLDING A TOY RABBIT (BELOW), WITH HER COUSIN ALICE CROMPTON, 1871

BEATRIX WITH HER PARENTS (RIGHT)

BEATRIX AND HER BROTHER BERTRAM (BELOW FRONT)

WITH PEN AND PAPER

In Victorian society, sketching and letter writing were considered to be essential accomplishments for every wellborn young lady, and were part of her first lessons at home. Beatrix Potter enjoyed both of these pastimes. Her earliest surviving sketchbooks date back to 1876, when she was nine. She was already drawing rabbits. Three letters from her childhood are addressed to her father. Beatrix would remain an avid letter-writer all her life.

Beatrix Potter's sketchbook in 1876 (left) shows Scottish scenery and imaginary rabbits with umbrellas, ice skates, and sleds.

A letter from Beatrix to her father (left):
"My dear Papa
I am not to go out in the garden as I have got a cold.
From your aff [affectionate daughter]
H B Potter"

IN THE SCHOOLROOM

Although Beatrix was six years older than her brother Bertram, they were very close. Apart from visiting cousins, they rarely met other children. The schoolroom was their world. When Bertram was six he was sent away to boarding school. Beatrix continued her education at home, with governesses. In 1881, at the age of 14, she began a secret journal in code. In it she recorded the many details of her world that caught her eye, and developed her style as a writer. Beatrix Potter the storyteller was learning her craft.

BEATRIX AND HER FIRST GOVERNESS, MISS DAVIDSON, 1877

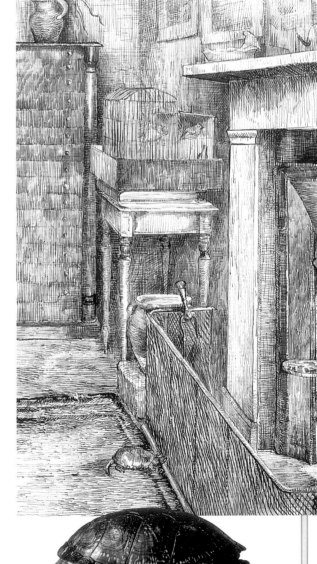

Beatrix drew this corner of the schoolroom (above right) in 1885. Her pet terrapin basks in front of the fire.

13

A Passion for Pictures

ALTHOUGH BEATRIX WAS OFTEN alone, she was not bored or unhappy. One reason was her love of art. Her parents liked to paint and they encouraged their children to do the same. Bertram would grow up to become an accomplished landscape painter. For Beatrix, they arranged for a drawing teacher to come to the house.

CARNATIONS BY
BEATRIX POTTER, AGED 14

Caricatures by Rupert Potter in 1853 (left) show that he shared his daughter's love of drawing and her sense of fun.

The English artist Millais (right) sat with his friend Rupert Potter (far right) while visiting the Potters in Scotland in 1880.

LIKE FATHER LIKE DAUGHTER

Rupert Potter's sketchbooks as a student are decorated with playful doodles, including dogs painting at an easel and playing the flute, and ducks in bonnets. Were his ducks the inspiration for his daughter's Jemima Puddle-duck 50 years later?

STILL LIFE BY
BEATRIX POTTER
(RIGHT), 1881

DRAWING LESSONS

Beatrix followed her teachers' instructions with a mixture of gratitude and frustration. She recorded her reservations in her journal for 1883. "I am convinced it lies chiefly with oneself ... Wish it did not cost so much, is the money being thrown away, will it even do me harm? ... Mrs. A. is very kind and attentive, hardly letting me do anything." Afterward Beatrix painted just as she liked.

HELEN POTTER'S BOX OF
WATERCOLOR PAINTS
AND BRUSHES

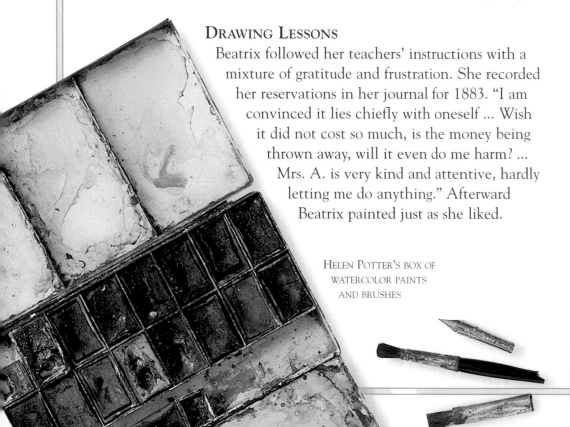

Victorian society flocked to art galleries such as
the Royal Academy in London, to see and be
seen at the latest exhibitions.

OLD MASTERS

Beatrix was 16 when her father first
took her to a major exhibition.
She described the paintings and her
excitement in her journal. "Been to
the Winter Exhibition of Old Masters
at the Academy. I had been looking
forward to it very much, but I never
thought it would be like this. I never
thought there *could* be such pictures."

EXPERT ENCOURAGEMENT

Photography was a relatively new art, but Rupert Potter was an
accomplished amateur. As well as taking landscapes and
family portraits, he photographed sitters for Sir John
Everett Millais, a leading British painter of the time.
Beatrix sometimes accompanied her father to Millais'
studio. He once paid her the greatest compliment, she
said, by telling her that "plenty of people can *draw*,
but you and my son John have observation."

*Beatrix was 10 when she drew this milkmaid
feeding ducks. She copied it from a collection
of nursery rhymes by the popular British
illustrator Walter Crane.*

*Among the illustrators whose work Beatrix knew
and admired were (above, from left to right) Kate
Greenaway, Randolph Caldecott, and Walter Crane.*

THE ART OF ILLUSTRATION

As a child, Beatrix pored over books such as *Alice in Wonderland* and
Uncle Remus. Later her father took her to see the latest works by top
illustrators. They made a lasting impression. In 1884, he bought two
drawings from Randolph Caldecott's *A Frog he would a-wooing go*.
Beatrix Potter's Mr. Jeremy Fisher of 1906 was a direct descendant.

THE WHITE RABBIT BY SIR JOHN
TENNIEL, FROM LEWIS CARROLL'S
ALICE IN WONDERLAND, 1865

THE ORIGINAL PETER RABBIT

BEATRIX POTTER AND HER BROTHER kept several pets in their schoolroom – rabbits, mice, birds, a bat, a frog, lizards, a terrapin, even a snake. Two rabbits were her particular favorites. The first was called Mr. Benjamin Bouncer, a rabbit of great character with an appetite for buttered toast and peppermints. The second was Peter Piper who, as Peter Rabbit, would be the hero of her first book.

Six heads of Benjamin Bunny, drawn in 1890, show how one rabbit's expressions can alter.

DRAWING PRACTICE

Beatrix taught herself a lot about drawing by studying her pets' anatomy and behavior and sketching them. To understand what gave animals their shape, Beatrix and Bertram also examined the skeletons of pets that had died.

This pet rabbit, sketched in 1880, is a predecessor of Benjamin H. Bouncer, also known as Bounce or Benjamin Bunny.

BEATRIX WITH BENJAMIN BUNNY ON A LEASH (BELOW), 1891

The Rabbit's Dream (left), c.1895, is of a comfy bed at Camfield Place, where Beatrix (and Peter) often stayed with her grandmother.

BEATRIX POTTER'S SKETCHBOOKS

FACT AND FANTASY

In *The Rabbit's Dream* (far left), Beatrix combined a realistic study of Peter Piper turning in his sleep with an affectionate illustration of his love of luxury. Later on her books, too, would combine fact with fantasy. Peter Piper lived to a great age, and died on January 26, 1901, aged nine.

RABBITS ON SHOW

Although Beatrix had grown up, she was expected to stay at home with her parents, as were all young women of her background. No wonder she enjoyed seeing friends. "Mrs. W. Bruce's children to tea, nice little girls but very shy. Peter Rabbit was the entertainment, but flatly refused to perform," then "caused shrieks of amusement by sitting up in the arm-chair and getting on to the tea-table."

JUDY THE PET LIZARD, 1884

PETER PIPER IN 1899 (ABOVE), ON HIS OLD QUILT IN FRONT OF THE FIRE

Beatrix drew other pets besides rabbits. Her dormouse Xarifa (above, 1887) was the sweetest little animal she knew.

Beatrix borrowed a friend's long-haired guinea pigs (right) as models for a card in 1893.

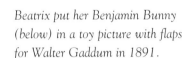

Beatrix put her Benjamin Bunny (below) in a toy picture with flaps for Walter Gaddum in 1891.

WALTER GADDUM, BEATRIX POTTER'S YOUNG COUSIN

ALL DRESSED UP

Beatrix often invented imaginary situations for her pets. In one of her "movable pictures" for young children, Benjamin Bunny is dressed as a grocer. (His son is hiding in a barrel, under a flap.) Other 19th-century artists showed animals in clothes, but few looked so convincing.

OFF TO THE COUNTRY

LIKE MANY VICTORIAN WOMEN, Beatrix led a very restricted life in London. Fortunately her parents enjoyed going on vacation, and rented a place in the country each summer. The whole household, complete with servants, carriages, and horses, would set off by train. Pets such as rabbits and lizards traveled in the family compartment, in specially-prepared boxes. Beatrix and her brother, released from Bolton Gardens at last, couldn't wait to explore the countryside.

BEATRIX ON A DONKEY, ON VACATION AT DALGUISE IN SCOTLAND, C. 1881

Stations such as Paddington in London could be crowded. The Potters avoided the crush by hiring a private compartment.

GETTING THERE
By the late 19th century, a network of railways crisscrossed the country. The Potter family took an omnibus from Bolton Gardens to the station. (Their spaniel Spot liked sitting on top – "he smiled benignly between his curls, and usually captivated the driver.") Their servants, carriages, and luggage had left a day or two before, to get everything ready and meet the family at the other end.

STABLES AT CAMFIELD PLACE (ABOVE), WITH BEATRIX IN THE FOREGROUND

STAYING AT GRANNY'S
Throughout the year, the Potters paid short visits to Rupert's parents at Camfield Place in Hertfordshire. It was less than a day's journey by coach from London, and big enough to house visiting relations (and their pets). Beatrix always slept in the No. 4 Bedroom. She loved the fresh air, rolling lawns, and hearty cooking. And she loved her grandmother's rambling tales of long ago.

BOAR FISH AT WEYMOUTH, 1895

SPRING AT THE SEASIDE
Each April, the Potters spent two weeks on the south coast for the sea air, light, and scenery. They filled their days with touring, photographing, and sketching. They stayed in hotels, which were not always a success – "it is possible to have too much Natural History in a bed," Beatrix wrote at Torquay in 1893. "What is to be thought of people who recommend near relations to an Hotel where there are bugs?"

SCOTTISH SUMMERS

For three months each summer, the Potter household headed north to Dalguise, a rented estate in Scotland. Beatrix and her brother explored the woods and riverbanks. Pets came too. "After breakfast," Beatrix wrote in her journal, "taking Mr. Benjamin Bunny to pasture at the edge of the cabbage bed with his leather dog-lead, I heard a rustling, and out came a little wild rabbit to talk to him."

Beatrix, Bertram, and their mother (below) on a beach in 1883. Mrs. Potter did not approve of swimming.

Rupert Potter photographed two fine salmon on the lawn at Dalguise in the 1870s (above), with Beatrix on the right.

Beatrix was nine when she carefully sketched the different species of caterpillar she found at Dalguise in 1875. She also made notes on their behavior.

SIDMOUTH BEACH (BELOW), PAINTED BY BEATRIX IN APRIL 1902

THE LAKE DISTRICT

In 1882, the Potters rented Wray Castle, overlooking Windermere in Cumbria. They returned every summer until 1892 and from 1896 onward. Beatrix immediately felt at home. "Went to Hawkshead on 19th. Had a series of adventures. Inquired the way three times, lost continually, alarmed by collies at every farm, stuck in stiles, chased once by cows." She was hooked.

A boating party at Windermere in the 1880s (right), with Betram in the bow on the left and Beatrix in the stern on the right.

"OLD MAN OF THE WOODS" FUNGUS (BELOW), 1893

THE YOUNG STORYTELLER

BEATRIX OFTEN GAVE her pictures of Peter, Benjamin, and others as presents to family and friends. She also sent illustrated letters to their children, with news of her pets. Young Freda Moore was told, "My rabbit is so hot he does not know what to do with himself. He has such thick fur, I think he would be more comfortable if he had a little coat" which he could take off.

PETER IN HIS COAT (ABOVE), FROM A PICTURE LETTER TO FREDA MOORE, 1897

Beatrix Potter's rabbit designs appeared first on greeting cards and then in a booklet called A Happy Pair (above), all printed by Hildesheimer & Faulkner in 1890.

A card designed by Beatrix in the shape of a coconut (right) reveals two mice inside, wishing you A Happy New Year. The top half of the coconut folds down to close the card.

FIRST SUCCESS

In 1890, Beatrix sold six rabbit designs for greeting cards for £6 ($29). "My first act was to give Bounce (what an investment that rabbit has been in spite of the hutches), a cupful of hemp seeds ... Then I retired to bed, and lay awake chuckling till 2 in the morning, and afterwards had an impression that Bunny came to my bedside in a white cotton night cap and tickled me with his whiskers."

RABBITS PULL CINDERELLA'S COACH TO THE BALL (BELOW), C. 1895

In a Christmas card printed by Hildesheimer & Faulkner (left) the mailman carries a big sack of mail – and a light snack.

A MYSTERIOUS DESIRE FOR MORE

The rabbit cards were a success. When their printer, Hildesheimer & Faulkner, asked for more, Beatrix and her uncle went to meet Mr. Faulkner. "Not one word did he say in praise of the cards, but he showed a mysterious desire for more ... He dwelt with peculiar fondness on some terrible cats, or rather little men with cat's heads stuck on their shoulders." Beatrix would do better.

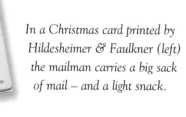

BENJAMIN BUNNY'S BOOKLET

Beatrix Potter's pet rabbit also featured in *A Happy Pair* (left), a booklet with illustrations by Beatrix and verse by Frederick E. Weatherly:

> "My name's Mister Benjamin Bunny,
> And I travel about without money,
> There are lots I could name,
> Do precisely the same,
> It's convenient, but certainly funny!"

Beatrix began to wonder whether she should write her own stories.

OUR DEAR RELATIONS (BELOW), OPENED AT A VERSE ILLUSTRATED BY BEATRIX (BELOW RIGHT), C. 1890

Beatrix produced six illustrations for the popular rhyme, Three Little Mice Sat Down to Spin (right), but she never had them printed.

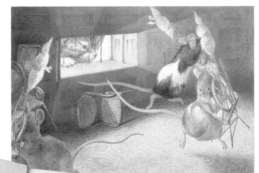

Dinner is served (above) is one of six scenes in The Rabbits' Christmas Party, c. 1892. This story without words was finally published as a fold-out panorama in 1987.

OLD FAVORITES

Beatrix enjoyed her success with booklets and cards, but she also continued to experiment with new drawing materials, techniques, and styles. In the 1890s she produced some of her most exquisite work, without any plans for publication. She was illustrating favorite nursery rhymes, fairy tales, and stories such as Joel Chandler Harris's *Uncle Remus* and Lewis Carroll's *Alice in Wonderland*.

BEATRIX POTTER'S *TRIAL OF THE KNAVE OF HEARTS* (RIGHT), 1894, FOR LEWIS CARROLL'S *ALICE IN WONDERLAND*

THE TALE OF PETER RABBIT

IN SEPTEMBER 1893, WHILE Beatrix Potter and her rabbit Peter Piper were on vacation in Scotland, a little boy she knew in London had a long illness. To cheer him up, Beatrix sent him a letter that told a story about Peter. "My dear Noel, I don't know what to write to you, so I shall tell you a story about four little rabbits whose names were – Flopsy, Mopsy, Cottontail and Peter."

FOUR LITTLE RABBITS – THE TALE BEGINS

... *"They lived with their mother in a sand bank under the root of a big fir tree.*

'Now, my dears,' said old Mrs Bunny 'you may go into the field or down the lane, but don't go into Mr McGregor's garden.'

Flopsy, Mopsy & Cottontail, who were good little rabbits went down the lane to gather blackberries, but Peter, who was very naughty ran straight away to Mr McGregor's garden and squeezed underneath the gate.

First he ate some lettuce, and some broad beans, then some radishes, and then, feeling rather sick, he went to look for some parsley; but round the end of a cucumber frame whom should he meet but Mr McGregor!

Mr McGregor was planting out young cabbages but he jumped up & ran after Peter waving a rake & calling out 'Stop thief'!

Peter was most dreadfully frightened & rushed all over the garden, for he had forgotten the way back to the gate. He lost one of his shoes among the cabbages and the other shoe amongst the potatoes. After losing them he ran on four legs & went faster, so that I think he would have got away altogether, if he had not unfortunately run into a gooseberry net and got caught fast by the large buttons on his jacket. It was a blue jacket with brass buttons, quite new."...

TO SEE HOW THE STORY
CONTINUES, TURN TO PAGE 24

A LASTING FRIENDSHIP

Beatrix Potter's last governess, Annie Carter, was only three years older than her pupil. They became good friends. Annie left to marry Edwin Moore in 1886. By 1893, when Beatrix sent her letter, they had five children – Noel was the eldest. Beatrix and her animals were their favorite visitors.

Annie, now Mrs. Moore, with her daughter Marjorie. Her bustling household must have been a welcome contrast to life at Bolton Gardens.

PETER CAUGHT FAST IN THE GOOSEBERRY NET

NOEL MOORE IN HIS SCHOOL UNIFORM, AGED 11

NOEL

Born on Christmas Eve, 1887, Noel Moore was five when Beatrix Potter sent him her new story about her rabbit Peter. She knew that Noel was devoted to him. Beatrix sent letters to all of the Moore children over the years, including at least 12 others to Noel. His sister Marjorie treasured her letters from Beatrix and kept them all, tied up with yellow ribbon.

ANOTHER STORY

Beatrix wrote Noel's letter at Eastwood, a house her father had rented for the summer on the Tay River in Perthshire, Scotland. That was on September 4, 1893. The next day she sent a letter to Noel's brother Eric, who was four.

"My dear Eric,
Once upon a time there was a frog called Mr. Jeremy Fisher, and he lived in a little house on the bank of a river..."

23

THE TALE CONTINUES

THE PETER RABBIT LETTER was a big hit with Noel and his family. As the years went by, Beatrix Potter's success in selling her drawings made her think it might be possible to do her own illustrated book. In 1900, she borrowed the letter back from Noel and copied it out to make a little black and white book. She added sections here and there, prepared 41 new illustrations, and had 250 copies printed in time for Christmas 1901.

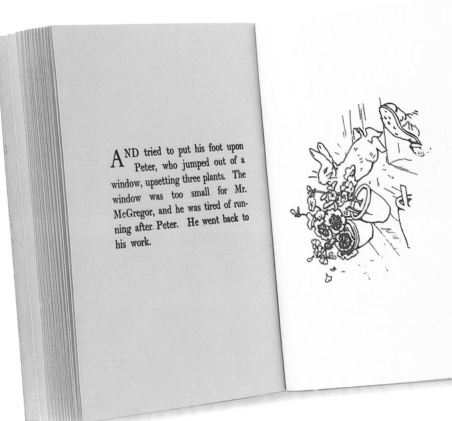

THE TALE IN PRINT

... *"PETER gave himself up for lost, and cried big tears; but his sobs were overheard by some friendly sparrows, who flew to him in great excitement, and implored him to exert himself.*

MR. MCGREGOR came up with a sieve, which he intended to pop upon the top of Peter; but Peter wriggled out just in time, leaving his jacket behind him,

AND rushed into the tool-shed, and jumped into a can. It would have been a beautiful thing to hide in, if it had not had so much water in it.

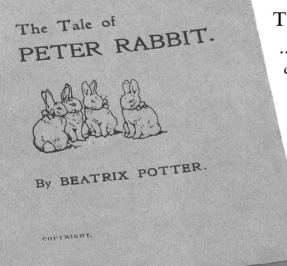

PRIVATELY PRINTED EDITION OF *THE TALE OF PETER RABBIT*, 1901

MR. MCGREGOR *was quite sure that Peter was somewhere in the tool-shed, perhaps hidden underneath a flower-pot. He began to turn them over carefully, looking under each. Presently Peter sneezed – 'Kertyschoo!' Mr. McGregor was after him in no time,*

AND *tried to put his foot upon Peter, who jumped out of a window, upsetting three plants. The window was too small for Mr. McGregor, and he was tired of running after Peter. He went back to his work.*

AND tried to put his foot upon Peter, who jumped out of a window, upsetting three plants. The window was too small for Mr. McGregor, and he was tired of running after Peter. He went back to his work.

In 1993, a facsimile of the private edition was printed in a limited edition of 750 copies, for Peter Rabbit's 100th birthday.

PETER sat down to rest; he was out of breath and trembling with fright, and he had not the least idea which way to go. Also he was very damp with sitting in that can.

AFTER a time he began to wander about, going lippity-lippity – not very fast, and looking all round.
He found a door in a wall; but it was locked, and there was no room for a fat little rabbit to squeeze underneath.

AN old mouse was running in and out over the stone door-step, carrying peas and beans to her family in the wood. Peter asked her the way to the gate, but she had such a large pea in her mouth that she could not answer. She shook her head at him. Peter began to cry again.

Beatrix drew The Rabbits' Potting Shed (*above*) in 1891 at Bedwell Lodge in Hertfordshire, where the Potters stayed that summer. Years later Beatrix said it was the setting for Mr. McGregor's shed.

In her picture of Peter by the locked door (*left*), Beatrix seems to pay tribute to fellow artist Anna Lea Merritt (1844–1930). She may have seen her work at the Royal Academy in London.

THEN he tried to find his way straight across the garden, but he became more and more puzzled. There surely never was such a garden for cabbages! Hundreds and hundreds of them; and Peter was not tall enough to see over them, and felt too sick to eat them. It was just like a very bad dream!

IN the middle of the garden he came to a pond where Mr. McGregor filled his water-cans. A white cat was staring at some goldfish; she sat very, very still, but now and then the tip of her tail twitched as if it were alive. Peter thought it best to go away without speaking to her; he had heard about cats from his cousin, little Benjamin Bunny." ...

THE TALE CONTINUES ON PAGE 26

LOVE LOCKED OUT
BY ANNA LEA MERRITT, 1889

THE TALE IS PUBLISHED

BEATRIX POTTER'S GOOD FRIEND Canon Rawnsley had written several books for children. He was convinced that her story was worth publishing and persuaded a publisher to look at it. Frederick Warne & Company decided that if Beatrix were willing to redraw all the pictures in color they would accept it. She agreed and the following year, in October 1902, *The Tale of Peter Rabbit* was published commercially for the first time.

A DOSE OF CAMOMILE TEA, ON THE TITLE PAGE

FIRST EDITION, 1902

PETER'S ESCAPE – A HAPPY ENDING

… "HE *went back towards the tool-shed, but suddenly, quite close to him, he heard the noise of a hoe – scr-r-ritch, scratch, scratch, scritch. Peter scuttered underneath the bushes. But presently, as nothing happened, he came out, and climbed upon a wheelbarrow, and peeped over. The first thing he saw was Mr. McGregor hoeing onions. His back was turned towards Peter, and beyond him was the gate!*

PETER *got down very quietly off the wheelbarrow, and started running as fast as he could go, along a straight walk behind some black-currant bushes.*

Mr. McGregor caught sight of him at the corner, but Peter did not care. He slipped underneath the gate, and was safe at last in the wood outside the garden.

77

1993 FACSIMILE OF THE FIRST EDITION

MR. MCGREGOR hung up the little jacket and the shoes for a scare-crow to frighten the blackbirds.

PETER never stopped running or looked behind him till he got home to the big fir-tree.

HE was so tired that he flopped down upon the nice soft sand on the floor of the rabbit-hole, and shut his eyes. His mother was busy cooking; she wondered what he had done with his clothes. It was the second little jacket and pair of shoes that Peter had lost in a fortnight!

I AM sorry to say that Peter was not very well during the evening. His mother put him to bed, and made some camomile tea; and she gave a dose of it to Peter!

'One table-spoonful to be taken at bed-time.'

BUT Flopsy, Mopsy, and Cotton-tail had bread and milk and black-berries for supper.

THE END"

86

In 2002, 100 years after the first edition of Peter Rabbit, Warne published a new one. In it they have reinstated six illustrations that were never used or were dropped to make room for the endpapers. The last of these shows Peter arriving home at the big fir tree (above).

CANON RAWNSLEY

The Potters met the Rawnsleys while on vacation at Wray Castle in the Lake District, and the two families became friends. Hardwicke Rawnsley was the minister for the village of Wray. He shared Beatrix Potter's love of the countryside, and encouraged her interest in conservation. He had a lasting influence on her work.

CANON RAWNSLEY AND YOUNG NOEL RAWNSLEY WITH BEATRIX IN THE LAKE DISTRICT C.1885

RHYMING PETER

Early educationalists and publishers believed that young children found reading easier and facts more memorable if their books were written in rhyme. Canon Rawnsley had enjoyed great success with his *Moral Rhymes for the Young*. He thought Warne might prefer *The Tale of Peter Rabbit* if it were in verse:

> **There were four little bunnies**
> **– no bunnies were sweeter**
> **Mopsy and Cotton-tail,**
> **Flopsy and Peter**

... and ended with a moral:

> **by far the best way**
> **[is] to do what we're told**
> **and our mothers obey.**

Warne preferred Beatrix Potter's prose.

A STAR IS BORN

BEATRIX POTTER'S PUBLISHER, Frederick Warne & Co., was run by Frederick's three sons. Beatrix dealt mainly with the youngest son, Norman. She became a frequent visitor to the company offices, driving there in the Potters' carriage and overseeing every detail of her book's design and production. Warne printed 8,000 copies to go on sale in October 1902. For Christmas they printed 20,000 more. Beatrix wrote to Norman in amazement, "The public must be fond of rabbits! What an appalling quantity of Peter."

BEATRIX POTTER'S EDITOR NORMAN WARNE, WITH HIS NEPHEW FRED

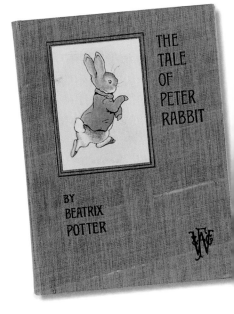

REPRINTED EDITION, WITH GREEN COVER INSTEAD OF BROWN, 1902

A HELPING HAND

Beatrix Potter's father took an avid interest in her new venture. She wrote to Warne to warn them that he might come with her to their offices to inspect her contract: "I think it is better to mention beforehand he is sometimes a little difficult; I can of course do what I like about the book being 36."

FREDERICK WARNE (SEATED ABOVE LEFT), FOUNDER OF THE FIRM

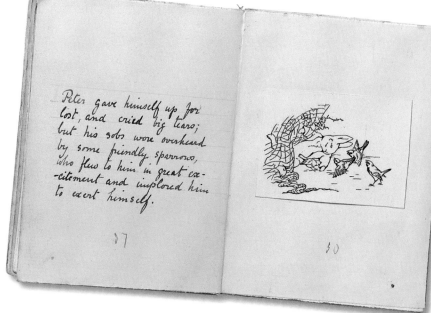

BEATRIX POTTER'S MANUSCRIPT FOR WARNE (ABOVE), WITH SKETCHES PASTED IN POSITION

STARTING AGAIN

Warne told their new author that "to make the book a success it is absolutely necessary that the pictures should be colored throughout." Beatrix promptly produced 41 new illustrations. Warne wanted only 30, so she had to shorten her story. A scene where Mr. McGregor sings *Three Blind Mice* as he hoes was cut – and saved for another book. So was Mrs. Rabbit knitting and selling lavender to feed and clothe her family.

To see how the new book would look, Beatrix colored in three pictures in a copy of her privately printed edition (left).

at Peter was
g the evening,
ing eaten too
or's garden.
im to bed, and
e tea;

POLISH! POLISH! POLISH!

In her search for the right word or phrase, Beatrix said, "I polish! polish! polish! – to the last revise!" She took the same care over her illustration and checked the quality of its reproduction and printing. She also thought about typefaces, bindings, cover designs, endpapers, title pages. The whole book, not just the story, was "By Beatrix Potter."

WARNE CATALOG FOR 1902–1903, STARRING PETER

OLD MRS. McGREGOR

Beatrix was never confident about drawing figures, and was not surprised when Warne asked her to redraw Mrs. McGregor.

NEW MRS. McGREGOR

LITTLE BOOKS FOR LITTLE HANDS

Beatrix wanted her books to be small, "to fit children's hands, not to impress grown-ups." Warne changed her format only very slightly, to 5¾ x 4 inches (144 x 110mm). All 23 of Beatrix Potter's Little Books are now that size.

PRICED AT ONE SHILLING

Beatrix wanted her books to be affordable: "all my little friends happen to be shilling people." *The Tale of Peter Rabbit* was published in October. The "shilling people" bought so many copies that Warne decided to put Peter on the front of its Christmas catalog. The naughty rabbit was already its biggest star.

Warne sold a standard edition with paper-covered boards for one shilling, and a deluxe edition with cloth and gold lettering (right) for one shilling and sixpence.

1/6

THE TALE OF PETER RABBIT

BY BEATRIX POTTER

BROWSING FOR THE PERFECT BOOK (ABOVE) AT A LONDON BOOKSTALL

THE TALE OF
THE TALE OF
THE TALE OF
THE TALE OF

THE TALE OF PETER RABBIT
THE TALE OF PETER RABBIT
THE TALE OF PETER RABBIT
THE TALE OF PETER RABBIT

PETER RABBIT'S FAN MAIL

FROM THE START, CHILDREN took Peter Rabbit to their hearts, and sent huge quantities of fan mail to Beatrix Potter. She always replied. Sometimes she sent picture letters with news and drawings of Peter. Sometimes she sent tiny letters in their own miniature envelopes. These were written as if by one of her animal characters, and they were addressed either directly to the child or to another character from the stories.

MINIATURE
LETTER TO
MASTER
DREW

Dear Master Drew
I am pleased to hear you like Miss Potter's books. Miss Potter is drawing pigs & mice. She says she has drawn enough rabbits. But I am to be put into one picture at the end of the pig book.
yr aff friend
Peter
× × × × × × ×

PRESENTS FOR PETER

Chidren often sent gifts with their letters. Louisa Ferguson's mother, in Wellington, New Zealand, sent a photograph of Louisa and a little bag. Beatrix sent back a picture letter decorated with drawings of Peter and his presents. "Dear little Louisa," it began, "It is a dear little bag and a dear little photograph! When I saw the bag I said 'This is for Peter Rabbit to carry his pocket handkerchief in!'"

PETER RABBIT (BELOW) SHOWS OFF
HIS NEW BAG FROM NEW ZEALAND

Master J. Ripley
Siddington Hall

Dear Mr Jackie,
  I am obliged to you for sending me a lovely calendar like a rose. I have tasted it and I think it is made of paper. So I shall not eat more of it, I shall hang it up in my rabbit hole!
      Love from your friend
  Peter Rabbit
  × × × × × ×

FOR
LONDON & PLACES
ABROAD
Next Collection
6.15 a.m.
Hours of Collection.
3.15 a. m.
9.   a. m.
1.   a. m.
4.   p. m.
6.   p. m.
12.   p. m.

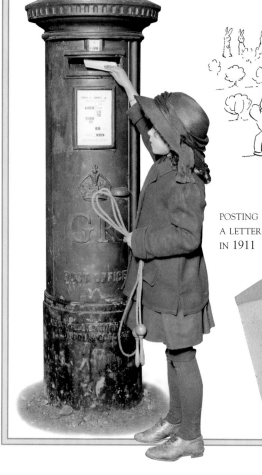

POSTING
A LETTER
IN 1911

When John Ripley sent a present, he got one thank-you letter from Peter (above) and another from Peter's mother, Mrs. Josephine Rabbit (right).

CHRISTMAS GREETINGS
FROM PETER RABBIT
AND FRIENDS (BELOW)

A Merry Christmas, Plenty of Buns!

from Cousin Benjamin

A merry Christmas!
from Tom Kitten

Master J. Ripley
Siddington Hall

Dear Mr Jackie,
  My son Peter has written to thank you for the roses, they will decorate my rabbit hole most elegantly, & I was in want of another calendar.

  Jos. Rabbit

P.S. I had not room to write my name properly.
      Josephine Rabbit
      × × × × ×

Master Drew
Kylemore.

Dear Master Drew

I am pleased to hear you like Miss Potter's books. Miss Potter is drawing pigs & mice. She says she has drawn enough rabbits. But I am to be put into one picture at the end of the pig book.

yr aff friend

Peter

× × × × × ×

Peter Rabbit writes to Andrew ("Drew") Fayle, of Dublin, Ireland – the "pig book" is The Tale of Pigling Bland, 1913.

A POSTBOX FOR LUCIE

Beatrix sent Lucie and Kathleen Carr, who lived in the Lake District, tiny tin models of postboxes for their letters. When Lucie was a baby, Beatrix sent her a copy of *Peter Rabbit*, inscribed "For Lucie with love from H.B.P., Christmas 1901 – I should like to put Lucie into a little book." (See page 59.)

THE MOORE CHILDREN, FROM RIGHT TO LEFT: NOEL, ERIC, MARJORIE, WINIFREDE, NORAH, JOAN, HILDA AND BEATRIX

PETER RABBIT'S POSTBAG

Back in 1893, Noel Moore had received the picture letter that first told the story of Peter Rabbit. Over the next 10 years, Beatrix sent dozens more to Noel and his brother and sisters. For miniature letters, she made the Moores a little mailbag marked "G.P.O." (General Post Office).

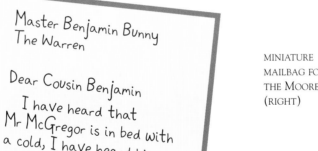

MINIATURE ENVELOPES WITH STAMPS IN RED CRAYON

Master Benjamin Bunny
The Warren

Dear Cousin Benjamin
I have heard that Mr McGregor is in bed with a cold, I have heard him sneezing half a mile off. Will you meet me at 6 this evening in the wood outside the garden gate?

In haste yr aff cousin

Peter Rabbit.

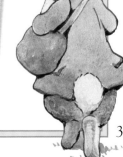

MINIATURE MAILBAG FOR THE MOORES (RIGHT)

John Ripley received two more miniature letters in 1909, from Peter Rabbit (left) and Mr. McGregor (below left).

MINIATURE MAILBOXES (ABOVE) FOR LUCIE AND KATHLEEN CARR

Master J. Ripley
Siddington Hall

Dear Mr Jackie,
I have had those there Rabbits in my garden again!

yrs respectfully

Mr McGregor

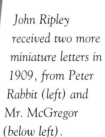

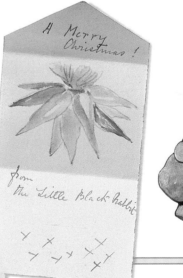

THE PETER RABBIT DOLL

"THERE IS A RUN on toys copied from pictures," Beatrix Potter noticed. She knew children loved rabbits, especially Peter Rabbit. Her new book was doing better than anyone expected. So she wrote to her editor, Norman Warne. "I am cutting out calico patterns of Peter, I have not got it right yet, but the expression is going to be lovely; especially the whiskers – (pulled out of a brush!)"

BEANIE PETER (BELOW AND TOP LEFT)

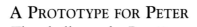

MRS. RABBIT

LIMITED EDITION PETER (ABOVE) MODELED ON BEATRIX POTTER'S ORIGINAL DESIGN

FLOPSY

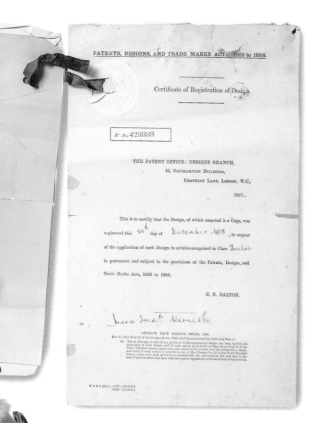

Beatrix photographed her Peter Rabbit doll (left) to register her copyright in 1903. It wasn't until 1993 that a limited edition of 2,500 dolls followed her design.

A PROTOTYPE FOR PETER

The challenge for Beatrix was to make her doll lifelike, appealing, and sturdy. "I think I will make one first of white velveteen painted," she wrote on December 10, 1903; "fur is very difficult to sew... I think I could make him stand on his legs if he had some lead bullets in his feet!" By December 15 it was ready. "I hope the little girl [Norman's niece, Winifred] will like the doll."

MR. McGREGOR

A RABBIT FROM GERMANY

While Beatrix urged Warne to do something about her doll, a German company offered her payment for the right to sell their rabbit dolls as Peter. But when she saw the dolls in the Harrods store in London, she was disappointed. "I find that Harrod's rabbits are *very ugly*," she told Norman Warne; "it was the color which made them so frightful, in combination with the shoes & coat." Not everyone disliked them, though. Beatrix also reported that "The rabbit dollies are in great force at Whitely's," another large London store. The "rabbit dollies" were here to stay.

A Peter Rabbit by Steiff of Germany c. 1904 (right) may be the same make that Beatrix saw in Harrods (during the store's expansion to its current size).

MOPSY   COTTON-TAIL   PETER

PLAYTIME WITH PETER

MR. MCGREGOR CHASES PETER all over again in a game devised by Beatrix in 1904. "I think this is rather a good game," she told Norman Warne. "I have written the rules at some length, (to prevent arguments!) but it is very simple, & the chances are strongly in favor of Peter." The aim of the game? "If Mr McGregor succeeds in getting upon the same square with Peter – then Peter is caught."

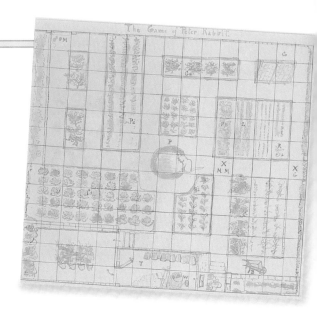

BEATRIX POTTER'S DESIGN FOR HER BOARD GAME (ABOVE RIGHT), 1904

GIANT WOODEN JIGSAW PUZZLE (LEFT), C. 1931

PETER RABBIT SLIPPERS AND LOG BOX, 1917

PIRATE MONEY BOX, UNLICENSED BY WARNE, C. 1920s

THE RACE IS ON

Warne revived the idea of a board game in 1917. It now involved other characters besides Peter and Mr. McGregor. Players took turns throwing dice and racing their characters to the finish line, with various setbacks along the way. Beatrix Potter's nieces liked the new version, and the game was a hit.

BEATRIX POTTER'S SIDESHOWS

Beatrix never tired of devising new "side-shows" – her term for merchandise to accompany her books. With Warne and with manufacturers, she considered everything from nursery wallpaper to china figurines and miniature tea sets, slippers and hot-water bottles, bibs and handkerchiefs, bookends and cookie tins. Today there are around 2,000 Beatrix Potter sideshows worldwide.

PATHS AND BURROWS GAME, 1988

PETER RABBIT'S RACE GAME (LEFT), 1919

HOT-WATER BOTTLE, C. 1950

COOKIE TIN, 1939

LEAD FIGURES FOR THE RACE GAME (ABOVE)

PART OF A CHINA TEA SET (BELOW), 1922

PETER RABBIT PLAYING CARDS (LEFT), 2000

MORE, PLEASE!

THE SUCCESS OF *PETER RABBIT*
led to more tales – concerning a
tailor, his cat Simpkin and some
mice, an impertinent squirrel, and
(back by popular demand) Peter
himself, this time accompanied by
his adventurous cousin Benjamin.

THE TAILOR OF GLOUCESTER

TIME WAS RUNNING OUT for young tailor John Prichard (1877–1934). He was making a new waistcoat for the Mayor of Gloucester, but as darkness fell he had to leave the unsewn pieces of cloth spread out on a table and go home. On his return to the shop in the morning he found to his amazement that the coat had been completed – by fairies, he supposed. They had run out of thread before they could finish the last button-hole, and left a tiny note saying, "NO MORE TWIST."

CAROLINE HUTTON

A NEW STORY

Beatrix Potter heard the tailor's story while staying near Gloucester with her cousin Caroline Hutton. She turned it into a fairy tale and sent it to Freda Moore for Christmas in 1901. "Because you are fond of fairy-tales and have been ill, I have made you a story all for yourself – a new one that nobody has read before. And the queerest thing about it – is that I heard it in Gloucestershire, and it is true!"

The Tailor of Gloucester lives in College Court, which Beatrix drew in 1897 on a hot summer day. In her Christmas story for Freda, it is covered in snow.

HOUSE OF THE
TAILOR OF
GLOUCESTER
(RIGHT) IN
COLLEGE COURT

Beatrix set her tale in the 18th century, "in the time of swords and periwigs and full-skirted coats." Her opening picture is based on Noon (above) by English artist William Hogarth (1697–1764).

In 1902, Beatrix borrowed Freda's story and redrew the pictures for a book. Little Percy Parton (right), the son of the Huttons' coachman, posed cross-legged as the Tailor of Gloucester.

THE TAILOR OF CHELSEA

On her return to London, Beatrix Potter came across a tailor's shop in Chelsea. She tore a button off her coat and went inside. While the tailor sewed the button back on, she studied his workshop so that she could fill her story with the authentic details of his trade. Later, when the story was turned into a book, Beatrix sent a copy to the Chelsea tailor.

The Tailor of Gloucester sits in the window of his shop, cross-legged on a table, from morning till dark.

TIPPETS FOR MICE

John Prichard was barely 20 when Beatrix heard his story. In her version he is an old man in spectacles, and very poor. He lives alone with his cat Simpkin in a house full of little brown mice. Every night, "worn to a ravelling," the tailor brings home snippets of leftover cloth, "tippets for mice and ribbons for mobs! for mice!"

"THERE WAS A SNIPPETING OF SCISSORS, AND SNAPPETING OF THREAD; AND LITTLE MOUSE VOICES SANG LOUDLY AND GAILY"

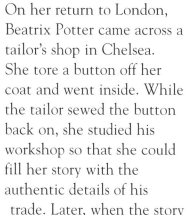

Beatrix sketched a kitchen hutch at the Huttons' home in Harescombe Grange (left). Laden with willow-pattern crockery, it was the perfect place for Simpkin to hide the mice he catches for his supper.

WINIFREDE ("FREDA") MOORE IN 1900

In 1902 Beatrix had her new story privately printed (right). A year later it was published by Warne.

The TAILOR OF GLOUCESTER.

BY BEATRIX POTTER.

Simpkin keeps his mice under the teacups and bowls and saucers. The tailor hears them tapping and lets them go. So Simpkin hides the last piece of twist in a teapot.

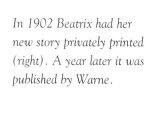

WHO LEFT THE NOTE?

In John Prichard's story, it was fairies who had helped finish the Mayor's new waistcoat in time for a grand procession. In Beatrix Potter's fairy tale, it was the mice. Some years later, John Prichard discovered that it was in fact his two kind-hearted apprentices.

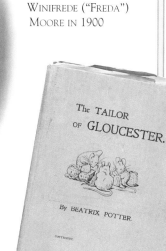

WAISTCOATS FOR MICE

BEATRIX POTTER'S MICE are as skillful with a needle and thread as the Tailor, and as grandly dressed as the Mayor. With stitches *so* neat and stitches *so* small, they sew together the Mayor's beautiful cherry-colored coat, made from corded silk and lined with taffetta, and his waistcoat of peach-colored satin embroidered with flowers. And they use the left-over snippets to make the same clothes in mouse-size miniature.

BEATRIX POTTER'S SKETCH OF THE COAT AT THE V&A

MUSEUM PIECES

Beatrix Potter found some of the inspiration for her new book at the South Kensington Museum (now the Victoria and Albert Museum, or V&A). She told her editor, Norman Warne, "I have been delighted to find I may draw some most beautiful 18th century clothes at S. Kensington museum." The clothes are still there.

MODEL MICE

Beatrix had often sketched mice in the past. But she wanted to study them again for her new drawings. "I have got some live mice," she wrote to Norman Warne from a vacation in Folkestone. A month later she was off to the Lake District. "But I will take the mice with me."

The mice are scientists in A Dream of Toasted Cheese *(left), 1899. Beatrix gave it to her uncle, a scientist, with a quotation from his latest work: "The peculiar pungent smell of this compound is noticed if we heat a bit of CHEESE in a test tube."*

While the tailor lies in bed with a fever the mice start work on the embroidered silk and satin, with one-and-twenty button-holes.

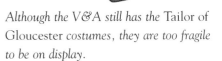

Although the V&A still has the Tailor of Gloucester costumes, they are too fragile to be on display.

Even the tiniest snippets make tippets (capes or stoles) for mice and ribbons for mobs (bonnets).

When Beatrix revised her story for Warne, she wrote it out in an exercise book and pasted in the illustrations. Some were cut out from her privately printed edition. Others were new, like this sketch for Simpkin (above).

READY FOR PUBLICATION
When Beatrix first sent Warne her story, she hoped they would not think it "very silly." After a year of cuts and revisions, Warne was so confident that it printed 20,000 copies to go on sale in October 1903. In December they had to print an extra 6,000 to keep up with demand. In her presentation copy from Warne, Beatrix later wrote, "This is my favourite amongst my little books."

For the deluxe edition's cloth binding (above), Beatrix found a pansy pattern from her grandfather's calico printworks.

HIGH PRAISE
When Beatrix Potter went back to see the tailor in Chelsea the following year, he told her he had shown his copy of the book to *The Tailor & Cutter* – the newspaper for tailors which the mouse on the bobbin is reading. The newspaper printed a review: "by far the prettiest story connected with tailoring we have ever read."

BEATRIX POTTER'S MINIATURE SEWING CASE (RIGHT)

The Tailor shouts for joy at the most beautifullest coat and waistcoat that ever were worn by a Mayor of Gloucester.

SQUIRREL NUTKIN

"THIS IS A TALE about a tail – a tail that belonged to a little red squirrel." So begins the story of Nutkin, an excessively impertinent squirrel who lives in a wood at the edge of a lake, with his brother Twinkleberry and the other squirrels. It is also the story of old Mr. Brown, an owl who lives in a hollow oak tree on an island in the middle of the lake. He does his best to ignore Nutkin – until one day Nutkin goes too far.

SQUIRRELS AFLOAT

Beatrix Potter first heard about the squirrels in 1897, on vacation in the Lake District. A lady living on Derwentwater wondered how they crossed the water to gather nuts on her island. In a picture letter to Eric Moore, Beatrix drew squirrels on rafts, using their tails as sails.

DERWENTWATER
SKETCHBOOK (BELOW), 1903

In the fall, when the nuts ripen, Nutkin and the other squirrels build little rafts of twigs and paddle away over the water to Owl Island.

A STORY FOR NORAH

In 1901, back in the Lake District on vacation, Beatrix sent the story of Nutkin in a letter to Norah Moore. She also showed it to Warne, which was eager to have another tale. She began to get ready, sketching squirrels, owls, and woods, and rewriting parts of the text.

Rupert Potter photographed Derwentwater (above) while on vacation in 1896, with old Mr. Brown's island in the middle.

BEWARE THE OWL

Unlike Nutkin, Beatrix and her brother Bertram knew better than to underestimate an owl. "We have got a tame owl," she wrote to Eric Moore in 1896; "he eats mice, he sits with a tail hanging out of his mouth."

The squirrels always bring old Mr. Brown a present, but Nutkin plagues him with riddles.

THEN ALL AT ONCE THERE WAS A FLUTTERMENT AND A SCUFFLEMENT AND A LOUD "SQUEAK!"

NUTKIN WRITES TO OLD MR. BROWN

Old Brown esq
Owl Island

Dear Sir,

   I should be exceedingly obliged if you will let me have back my tail. I will gladly pay 3 bags of nuts for it, if you will please post it back to me, I have written twice Mr Brown. I think I did not give my address, it is Derwent Bay Wood.

yrs respectifully

Sq. Nutkin

SCELL NUSKIN

Old Mr. Brown may have had his doubts, but the public adored Nutkin. *The Tale of Squirrel Nutkin* went on sale in August 1903. Within weeks, children were writing to Beatrix about "Scell nuskin" – "it seems an impossible word to spell," she told Norman Warne, "but they say they have 'red' it right through and that it is 'lovely.'" By Christmas her father found a toy squirrel that was already being sold as Nutkin.

TOY "NUTKIN" MADE BY
FARNELL & CO., C. 1903

43

THE LAKE DISTRICT

BEATRIX FIRST VISITED the English Lake District when she was 16 and her father rented Wray Castle on Windermere. In the years that followed, the Potters spent many more summers by Windermere or another lake, Derwentwater. Beatrix loved the countryside there. It became the setting for the world of Peter Rabbit and his friends.

Rupert Potter photographed his family on the lawn at Wray Castle, on their first vacation in the Lake District. Their spaniel, Spot, was there too.

BEATRIX POTTER (ABOVE) IN HER CARRIAGE NEAR WINDERMERE, 1889

BACKGROUND SKETCH FOR THE EDGE OF THE LAKE WHERE NUTKIN AND THE OTHER SQUIRRELS MAKE THEIR RAFTS

BACKGROUND SKETCH FOR OWL ISLAND (RIGHT) WHERE THE SQUIRRELS GO TO GATHER NUTS

DERWENTWATER

Squirrel Nutkin is set in Derwentwater. The Potters rented two houses on the western side, Lingholm and Fawe Park. From there Beatrix set out to explore Nutkin's woods along the shore, St. Herbert's Island (home to old Mr. Brown), and the Cat Bells hills and Newlands Valley beyond.

THE THREE-IN-ONE SKETCHBOOK

In the summer of 1903, while staying at Fawe Park, Beatrix was working on three tales. Her sketchbook includes backgrounds for all three. She lists them on the final page:
"*Mrs. Tiggy-Winkle* Newlands
Fawe Park   *Benjamin Bunny*
Derwentwater   *Squirrel Nutkin*."

SIGHTSEEING

Beatrix enjoyed walking along the shore or up in the hills. There were other excursions, too. A steamboat ferried passengers across Derwentwater to the far side of the lake. The family carriage took the Potters to local market towns and historic sites. Beatrix could take the pony and carriage for short drives, to visit people, or simply to enjoy the fresh air and scenery. Her journals and her books are full of little details she noticed along the way.

PORTRAIT OF CANON RAWNSLEY BY FREDERICK YATES, 1915

FAWE PARK (ABOVE), WHERE THE POTTERS STAYED IN 1903

DERWENTWATER FROM LINGHOLM (RIGHT), PHOTOGRAPHED BY RUPERT POTTER IN 1906

PROTECTING THE LAKES

Visitors can still walk in Beatrix Potter's footsteps and admire the same views – thanks in part to her friend, Canon Rawnsley. In 1895 he helped set up the National Trust to preserve the local landscape and way of life. Beatrix was an early supporter, and the Trust continues its work to this day.

BACKGROUND SKETCH FOR THE OVERHANGING BRANCH WHERE THE SQUIRRELS LOAD THEIR RAFTS WITH SACKS OF NUTS

BACKGROUND SKETCH FOR THE TREE STUMP (RIGHT) WHERE NUTKIN PLAYS MARBLES

DERWENTWATER TODAY

PETER RABBIT RETURNS

PETER HAD NARROWLY ESCAPED **Mr. McGregor's** clutches (and **Mrs. McGregor's** pie dish) at the end of *The Tale of Peter Rabbit*, but his clothes were still in the possession of Mr. McGregor's scarecrow. And so the scene was set for a sequel. Peter, this time accompanied by his adventurous little cousin Benjamin Bunny, returns to the garden to rescue his property.

OVER THE WALL AND INTO THE GARDEN

The first time Peter broke into Mr. McGregor's garden, he squeezed under a gate. This time Benjamin takes him up onto the garden wall. "It spoils people's clothes to squeeze under a gate," he says; "the proper way to get in, is to climb down a pear tree." The pear trees and the wall are at Fawe Park, which overlooks Squirrel Nutkin's Derwentwater.

There is rainwater in Peter's shoes and his coat is somewhat shrunk. Benjamin tries on Mr. McGregor's old tam-o-shanter, but it is too big for him.

A REAL GARDEN

Beatrix Potter stayed at Fawe Park in 1903, while on vacation with her family. The garden was the perfect setting for her new bunny book. At the end of the summer Beatrix told Norman Warne, "I think I have done every imaginable rabbit background, & miscellaneous sketches as well – about 70!"

Fawe Park's garden wall is the first drawing in Beatrix Potter's Derwentwater sketchbook of 1903, which also contains sketches for Nutkin.

Wooden planks (right) make a path across the cabbage patch for the gardener (and visiting rabbits).

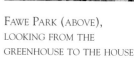

FAWE PARK (ABOVE), LOOKING FROM THE GREENHOUSE TO THE HOUSE

46

OLD MR. BENJAMIN BUNNY
PRANCING ALONG THE TOP OF THE WALL

Underneath the basket it was quite dark, and the smell of onions was fearful; it made Peter Rabbit and little Benjamin cry.

TRAPPED!

Before they leave, the two cousins take a detour through the onions and lettuces. Peter keeps hearing noises. Benjamin is perfectly at home – until they run into Mr. McGregor's cat. They hide under a basket. The cat sits on top, for *five hours*. Luckily Benjamin's father old Mr. Bunny comes to the rescue.

SKETCH OF A SWILL – A BASKET FOR LIGHT LOADS SUCH AS WEEDS FROM THE BORDER OR ONIONS FOR THE POT

PETER RABBIT WRITES TO BENJAMIN BUNNY

Master Benjamin Bunny
The Warren

Dear Cousin Benjamin
    I have heard that Mr. McGregor is in bed with a cold, I have heard him sneezing half a mile off. Will you meet me at 6 this evening in the wood outside the garden gate?
    In haste yr aff cousin

Peter Rabbit

BENJAMIN THE BRAVE

The original Benjamin, Beatrix said, "was a very handsome tame Belgian rabbit… extremely fond of hot buttered toast, he used to hurry into the drawing room when he heard the tea-bell!" Benjamin was also "an abject coward, but believes in bluster, could stare our old dog out of countenance, [and] chase a cat that has turned tail."

In 1908, Beatrix sent a photograph of her pet rabbit Benjamin (right) as a postcard to young Master Jack Ripley in Argentina.

MORE ABOUT MR. MCGREGOR

CERAMIC OF
MR. MCGREGOR

ALTHOUGH NUMEROUS GARDENS CLAIM to be **Mr. McGregor's** garden, no single, definite location has ever been established. In response to her readers enquiries, Beatrix Potter herself wrote that "the backgrounds of Peter Rabbit are a mixture of locality" and that "Mr. McGregor was no special person." All that is certain is that Beatrix loved gardens.

ANOTHER GARDENER (RIGHT), MR. JESSE BUCKLAND, C. 1912

Beatrix drew this rabbit in 1891 (left), two years before the Peter Rabbit letter, while staying at Bedwell Lodge, Hertfordshire.

MR. MCGREGOR'S ROOTS

His name and his tam-o-shanter suggest Mr. McGregor must have been Scottish. Beatrix was on vacation in Scotland when she first wrote the Peter Rabbit story. And the house where she was staying was rented for the summer from a man called Mr. Macgregor.

RARE GLIMPSE OF MRS. MCGREGOR (RIGHT), IN THE TALE OF THE FLOPSY BUNNIES

GARDENS BEATRIX KNEW

Beatrix sketched all kinds of gardens on her travels. Big country houses had kitchen gardens for vegetables, fruits, and flowers, with a high wall to keep out winds (and intruders). They also had formal gardens landscaped with trees, lawns, and ponds. Cottage gardens were smaller but packed with blooms. Some had separate plots for fruits and vegetables.

WALLED GARDEN (ABOVE), POSSIBLY IN THE LAKE DISTRICT AT LAKEFIELD, SAWREY, C. 1900

MRS. MCGREGOR'S PIE

Mr. McGregor's wife appears only three times in Beatrix Potter's 23 tales. Once encountered, never forgotten. In the first tale, Peter's mother warns her children, "don't go into Mr. McGregor's garden: your Father had an accident there; he was put in a pie by Mrs. McGregor."

WALL AT MELFORD HALL IN SUFFOLK, WHERE BEATRIX STAYED WITH COUSINS

Beatrix first saw Mr. McGregor's lily pond (and cat, right) when she stayed in Tenby, Wales, in April 1900.

MR. McGREGOR'S YEAR

Beatrix Potter knew that gardeners have to work hard all through the year to grow food to eat and flowers to admire. Here is a reminder for Mr. McGregor about just some of the essential tasks that keep him busy throughout the tales, from winter right through to the fall. The last thing he needs is another visit from Peter Rabbit and Benjamin Bunny.

WINTER

1. START NOW – it's cold outside but you can get ahead by sowing seeds in the greenhouse.

CLAY POTS

2. When your seedlings sprout, pot them or move them to the cold frame outdoors.

SPRING

RAKE

10. Clean up the garden for winter – rake up the leaves and have a bonfire.

FALL

9. Time to pick blackberries, apples, and other fall crops.

DIBBER

3. Plant out your seedlings in the garden – use a dibber to punch holes in the ground.

BLACKBIRD

4. Put up a scarecrow to keep greedy blackbirds away.

8. Mow the lawns and put the grass cuttings on the compost heap.

LAWNMOWER

SUMMER

7. It's hot – don't forget to water the garden and keep the pond filled up.

GOOSEBERRIES

WATERING CAN

HOE

6. Hoe the weeds or else they'll choke everything you've planted.

5. Put netting on the gooseberry bushes too.

TWO BAD MICE

TOM THUMB AND HUNCA MUNCA, the two bad mice, explore a beautiful dolls' house and get up to mischief while the dolls are away. They were named after two of Beatrix Potter's pets. The dolls' house was based on one her editor, Norman Warne, built for his niece Winifred. Norman also made a special "mouse house" for the real Hunca Munca, with a glass side so that Beatrix could watch and draw her.

FLAT IRON

Was this doll the model for fair-haired Lucinda? Like Hunca Munca, Beatrix Potter was a great hoarder and collected antique dolls, old English furniture and china, and more besides.

OUT OF BOUNDS

Beatrix was invited to visit the Warnes to sketch Winifred's new dolls' house, but Mrs. Potter disapproved of Beatrix going to their house. She wrote to apologize: "my mother is so 'exacting' ... It does wear a person out." So that Beatrix could finish her sketches, Norman sent her photographs instead.

SHOPPING FOR DOLLS

For inspiration, Norman sent Beatrix two dolls, and then some furniture and food from a London toystore, Hamleys. "I received the parcel from Hamley's this morning," she wrote back. "The ham's appearance is enough to cause indigestion. I am getting almost more treasures than I can squeeze into one small book."

Winifred Warne and the dolls' house made for her by Norman Warne in 1904 – "the kind of house where one cannot sit down without upsetting something," Beatrix said, "I know the sort!"

IN THE MOUSE HOUSE

The real Hunca Munca liked her new house. "I stopped her in the act of carrying a doll as large as herself up to the nest," Beatrix told Norman, "she cannot resist anything with lace or ribbon; (she despises the dishes)."

The dolls' house belongs to two dolls, Lucinda and Jane. They buy their food ready-made, as the Two Bad Mice are about to find out...

The mice discover that the dolls' food is rock-hard and stuck to the plates. They hurl it to the floor – bang, bang, smash, smash!

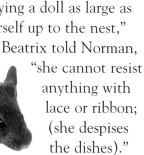

MINIATURE CUTLERY
FOR DOLLS – OR
HUNGRY MICE

DOLLS' HOUSE FOOD
FROM HAMLEYS

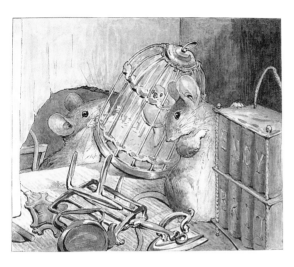

NOT SO NAUGHTY AFTER ALL

Beatrix ends her tale by reconciling her readers' sense of justice to her characters' true nature. Mice can't help being mice. So the little girl who owns the dolls' house gets a policeman doll (like Winifred's) to guard against future burglars. Her nurse sets a mousetrap. The mice, though unrepentant, find a way to show the dolls their gratitude.

WICKER CRADLE,
PERFECT FOR HUNCA
MUNCA'S BABIES

Hunca Munca has a frugal mind. With Tom Thumb's assistance she takes some odds and ends from the dolls' house.

Beatrix later got a dolls' house of her own (below) and filled it with the furniture for Two Bad Mice, plus miniature portraits of Winifred and her sister.

SAUCEPAN

KETTLE

TWO BAD MICE WRITE TO ANDREW FAYLE

Dear Drew,
  This is love from lots of little mice, sent by
  Tom Thumb
  & Hunca Munca.

  x x x x x x x x x

A New Life for Beatrix

1905 WAS AN IMPORTANT YEAR for Beatrix Potter. Now that she was earning a regular income from her books she decided to buy a house of her own. She chose a farm called Hill Top in the Lake District village of Near Sawrey. That same year her publisher, Norman Warne, with whom she had worked closely on all her books, asked her to marry him. Beatrix was very happy to accept. Her life seemed set to change.

FRONT DOOR KEY FOR HILL TOP, AND OLD COIN THAT BEATRIX FOUND THERE

The Perfect Place

Beatrix first got to know Sawrey in 1896, when she and her family spent the summer at Lakefield, a house on the edge of the village. She thought Sawrey was "as nearly perfect a little place as I ever lived in." Hill Top would provide her with an escape from her parents' house, and with inspiration for her next books.

Beatrix found these marbles in a wall while renovating Hill Top. She kept them with a note that explains she also found a George III coin in the front-door keybox. For 100 years or so, the coin had prevented anyone from turning the key to lock the door.

Beatrix sketched her new house c. 1905. Later she added a wing for the previous tenants, the Cannons, who stayed on to look after the farm for her.

Secret Engagement

Beatrix was allowed to wear Norman's ring but not to announce her engagement, which appalled her parents. In their eyes, he was her social inferior. Publishing was a trade, not a profession, so the son of a publisher was an unsuitable match for the daughter of a lawyer. Besides, if Beatrix married, who would look after them in their old age?

WARNES CUTTING A DASH ON BICYCLES – NORMAN IS ON THE FAR LEFT

TRAGEDY

On August 25, one month after Norman had proposed to Beatrix, he died from a sudden illness, aged 37. Beatrix was devastated and buried herself in her next book, *The Tale of Mrs. Tiggy-Winkle*. As she explained to Harold Warne, Norman's brother and now her editor, "I feel as if my work and your kindness will be my greatest comfort."

Beatrix drew Bedford Square, London, at dusk (above) while staying with the Warnes after Norman's death.

HILL TOP AT NIGHT IN SNOW (RIGHT), C. 1910

Hill Top today (above). The village of Near Sawrey lies just behind the trees, with Esthwaite Water and the Langdale Pike hills beyond.

HILL TOP IN THE FALL (BELOW), FROM BEATRIX POTTER'S SKETCHBOOK FOR 1905

RETREAT

From now on, Beatrix spent as much time as possible at Sawrey, overseeing the renovations to Hill Top. She told Millie Warne, Norman's sister and her close friend, that the house "really is delightful if the rats could be stopped out!" and added that "'Tabitha Twitchit' [the farm cat] is so extremely pleased to see me, I am afraid she is pleased *not* to see the hedgehog [Beatrix Potter's pet, Mrs. Tiggy], which she disliked."

PETER RABBIT'S FRIENDS

THE PETER RABBIT BOOKS
were now an established series.
Enter Mrs. Tiggy-winkle and other
new characters. Their tales are set
in the same beautiful countryside
as Hill Top, Beatrix Potter's new
home in the Lake District.

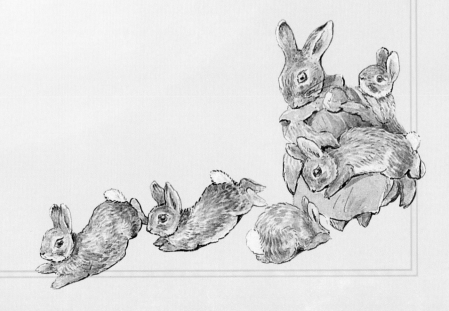

PETER RABBIT'S WORLD

PETER RABBIT'S INSTANT POPULARITY started Beatrix Potter on a long career as an author and she went on to write many other stories. They were collected together in a series known as *The Original Peter Rabbit Books*, a set of 23 little volumes, all featuring animal characters. Beatrix Potter grew up in the city but loved the countryside – the world of Peter Rabbit and his friends recreates the charm of an English country community.

MRS. TIGGY-WINKLE

THE HILLSIDE
High up in the hills are streams and gorse bushes – perfect for washing clothes and hanging them out to dry.

THE VILLAGE
Everyone knows one another in the village. They invite their neighbors to tea, and gossip at the shop. And they like to keep their pretty cottages and gardens looking their best, for some neighbors can be critical.

GINGER AND PICKLES

RIBBY

DUCHESS

KEP THE COLLIE

SAMUEL WHISKERS

LITTLE PIG ROBINSON (WHO LIVED ON A FARM IN DEVON BEFORE HE WENT TO SEA)

THE LAKE
There's nowhere nicer to go out in a boat for a bit of fishing. Look out for frogs among the lily pads.

THE FARM
Sheep, pigs, cows, and horses come into the farmyard for shelter. Ducks and hens have nesting boxes there. Rats and mice raid the barns for grain. Working dogs and cats live out in the yard too. Their more pampered cousins live in the farmhouse as pets.

MR. JEREMY FISHER

THE WOODS

Away in the woods, squirrels, owls, and other animals live in lofty oaks and beech trees. Rabbits outnumber them all, and feature in many of the tales. Peter and his relatives live in burrows under banks and tree roots, but often venture into nearby fields and gardens for tasty treats. Foxes and badgers dig their sets deep underground. They are partial to rabbits, and to farmyard ducks and hens.

PETER RABBIT

OLD MR. BROWN

MRS. TITTLEMOUSE

A FIERCE BAD RABBIT

TOMMY BROCK

TIMMY TIPTOES

CECILY PARSLEY

MR. TOD

JEMIMA PUDDLE-DUCK

THE FLOPSY BUNNIES

SQUIRREL NUTKIN

BENJAMIN BUNNY

THE TOWN

In the townhouses of London, Gloucester, and the Lake District's Hawkshead, there are rich pickings for mice – and for cats! Farm animals only ever go to town on market day – or by mistake, like Timmy Willie.

PIGLING BLAND

TOM KITTEN

TIMMY WILLIE, A COUNTRY MOUSE

JOHNNY TOWN-MOUSE

THE TAILOR OF GLOUCESTER

MISS MOPPET

APPLEY DAPPLY

TWO BAD MICE

MRS. TIGGY-WINKLE

A LITTLE GIRL CALLED LUCIE visits Peter Rabbit's world in the *The Tale of Mrs. Tiggy-Winkle*. Lucie is searching for her lost handkerchiefs and comes across a mysterious little door in the hillside. It opens into a kitchen with a flagstone floor, wooden beams, and furniture, just like any other Lake District kitchen, but in miniature. It belongs to Mrs. Tiggy-winkle, who does the washing for all the animals.

COVERED IN PRICKLES

Mrs. Tiggy-winkle is very stout, short, and prickly. Beatrix told Norman Warne that her pet hedgehog Mrs. Tiggy was the model – "so long as she can go to sleep on my knee she is delighted, but if she is propped up on end for half an hour, she first begins to yawn pathetically, and then she *does* bite! Never the less, she is a dear person."

STUDIES OF A HEDGEHOG'S HEAD, PRESUMABLY THE TAME MRS. TIGGY'S, 1904

IN THE HILLS

Mrs. Tiggy-winkle's home is somewhere high in the Cat Bells, which overlook Derwentwater to the east, Little Town and Newlands Valley to the west and southwest. Lucie takes a winding path from the valley up the hillside. Beatrix often brought her paintbox and camera up here, and now hillwalkers from around the world make the same trek.

VIEW FROM CAT BELLS (ABOVE) DOWN TO NEWLANDS VALLEY

In the Derwentwater sketchbook of 1903 (left), Beatrix painted Lucie's path up from Newlands Valley to Cat Bells.

"THAT ONE BELONGS TO OLD MRS. RABBIT; AND IT DID SO SMELL OF ONIONS!"

BENJAMIN BUNNY'S JACKET

FLOPSY BUNNY'S CAPE

LUCIE'S HANKY

PETER RABBIT'S JACKET

COCK ROBIN'S WAISTCOAT

MRS. TIGGY-WINKLE'S CAP

THE REAL LITTLE LUCIE

Lucie was the daughter of the Vicar of Newlands. Beatrix knew the family well and dedicated the book to "The real little Lucie of Newlands." Lucie finds her hankies (and her pinafore) and goes back down the path with Mrs. Tiggy-winkle to deliver the rest of the laundry to the animals.

LUCIE (WITH CAT) AND HER SISTER KATHLEEN CARR

SKETCH OF A LAKE DISTRICT KITCHEN, WITH LAUNDRY, 1905

A REAL WASHERWOMAN

On vacation in Scotland, the Potters had their laundry done by Kitty MacDonald. "She is a comical, round little old woman, as brown as a berry," Beatrix wrote in her journal in 1892, "and wears a multitude of petticoats and a white mutch [a linen cap]." Twenty years later, Mrs. Tiggy-winkle looked much the same.

Like all gentlemen of the time, Tom Titmouse was "most terrible particular" and liked Mrs. Tiggy-winkle to dip his best shirts in liquid starch after washing. The starch stiffened as the shirt was dried and ironed, which kept it wrinkle-free.

After the wash, Mrs. Tiggy-winkle hangs up all kinds and sizes of clothes to air, including a very shrunken blue jacket belonging to Peter Rabbit.

MR. JEREMY FISHER WRITES TO MRS. TIGGY-WINKLE

Mrs Tiggy Winkle
Cat Bells

Mr J. Fisher regrets to have to complain again about the washing. Mrs. T. Winkle has sent home an enormous handkerchief marked "D. Fayle" instead of the tablecloth marked J.F.

If this continues every week, Mr J. Fisher will have to get married, so as to have the washing done at home.

THE PIE AND THE PATTY-PAN

IN THE VILLAGE OF SAWREY, an invitation is an event. *The Tale of the Pie and The Patty-Pan* is set there and tells what happens when Ribby the cat invites the little dog Duchess to an elegant tea party. But even when they wish to behave with the utmost politeness, dogs and cats don't always share the same tastes. This leads to unexpected trouble.

CERAMIC FIGURINE OF RIBBY

TEATIME TREATS

In Beatrix Potter's day, afternoon tea with friends was a part of every lady's social calendar. Beatrix and her mother continually issued and received invitations to tea. It was a formal meal. Young and old were stylishly dressed and on their best behavior. Fine china, silver, and linen were used. And pets did tricks for titbits from the table.

Ribby's invitation promises something so very nice, in a pie dish with a pink rim. The more Duchess reads the letter, the more she fears it will be mouse pie.

Duchess's front garden still blooms today, at Buckle Yeat in Sawrey village. The twin gateposts are carved from local stone.

BEATRIX POTTER'S EDWARD VII CORONATION TEAPOT, 1901

SAWREY SETTINGS

The new Tale was longer than usual and needed more illustrations. Beatrix did some in color and some in black-and-white, which took less time. Duchess and Ribby's homes were inspired by the cottages and gardens she knew from vacations in Sawrey. She sketched Duchess's front garden at Buckle Yeat and her front door at the Post Office. Ribby's front porch and parlor were at Lakefield Cottage. Ribby's oven, teapot, and water pump came from Beatrix Potter's own house at Hill Top.

Under an arch in Hawkshead (above), Ribby and Duchess happen to meet each other – Ribby with her shopping basket, Duchess with her pie.

BEFORE THE TEA PARTY

Duchess cannot offend Ribby by refusing mouse pie. So she bakes a veal and ham pie in an identical dish, with a patty-pan inside. She puts her pie in Ribby's bottom oven while Ribby is out shopping.

When the two friends sit down for tea, the pie proves extremely toothsome. But where is the patty-pan? Has Duchess swallowed it?

VEAL AND HAM PIE,
OR IS IT?

POLITE CONVERSATION

When Beatrix sent Norman Warne her new story early in 1905, she added, "There is one thing in its favour, children like conversations." Duchess and Ribby exchange the pleasantries Beatrix had heard over countless tea tables. Snobby Tabitha Twitchit is less polite when she hears her cousin Ribby has invited a dog to tea instead of her. "The very idea!"

Tabitha Twitchit's shop is in Hawkshead (above), the market town near Sawrey. Tabitha stocks tea, marmalade, and sugar.

RIBBY LEAVING TABITHA
TWITCHIT'S SHOP

A patty-pan (below) holds up the pastry crust on top. That stops the pastry from sinking when the pie is taken out of the oven and begins to cool.

MRS. ROGERSON WITH "MIDDY," A
DESCENDANT OF "DUCHESS", 1940

TWO MODELS FOR DUCHESS

Duchess brushes her coat to look her best for tea. She is a pedigree Pomeranian, with a fine ruff of fur. Beatrix knew two "Poms" in Sawrey, owned by Mrs. Rogerson. "Darkie" had a handsome black coat, but "Duchess" was more intelligent. Like her namesake, she could sit up and balance a sugar lump on her nose.

RIBBY SENDS DUCHESS ANOTHER INVITATION

Mrs Duchess
Belle Green

My dear Duchess,
    If you are not engaged will you come to tea tomorrow? but if you are away I shall put this in the post and invite cousin Tabitha Twitchit. There will be a red herring, & muffins & crumpets.
    The patty pans are all locked up. Do come.
        yr aff friend
        Ribby.

COME TO TEA

PETER RABBIT'S FRIENDS like nothing better than a party. Mostly traditional country fare is served, though the ingredients are adapted to suit each animal's tastes. Some hosts are not to be trusted – Jemima Puddle-duck's foxy gentleman is planning to eat her. But mostly the tales reflect the menus and manners of a genteel world Beatrix Potter knew well.

PETER RABBIT
COOKIE TIN,
1939

ROASTED GRASSHOPPER,
WHICH FROGS CONSIDER
A BEAUTIFUL TREAT

GOOD LITTLE BUNNIES HAVE BREAD AND
MILK AND BLACKBERRIES FOR SUPPER

ONE OF THE
TAILOR OF
GLOUCESTER'S
PRETTY CHINA
TEA CUPS

DRESSING FOR DINNER
Beatrix Potter's father and his friends always dressed for dinner, as all gentlemen did – even on a fishing vacation. When Mr. Jeremy Fisher comes home after a bit of fishing, he invites two friends to dine on roasted grasshopper with ladybug sauce. Jeremy and Sir Isaac Newton wear their best waistcoats and cravats. Alderman Ptolemy Tortoise wears his chain of office.

IN THE NURSERY
Some of the tales hint at Beatrix Potter's childhood memories of mealtimes in her London nursery. When naughty Peter returns from Mr. McGregor's garden, his mother sends him to bed. Flopsy, Mopsy, and Cotton-tail, who are good little bunnies, put on their bibs and have bread and milk and blackberries for supper. Little Beatrix and her brother must have had similar treats.

CAKE PLATE
C. 1850, FOR AN
ELEGANT TEA PARTY

From the nursery onward, ladies entertained their friends with polite conversation and fine china for tea.

FLOWERS
AND
FRUIT
DECORATE
THE TABLE FOR
A 19TH-CENTURY
DINNER PARTY

SIMPLE FARE

Beatrix loved the hearty country cooking at her grandmother's house in Hertfordshire. Her parents' menus in London were more elaborate, with the sort of dishes the Two Bad Mice find in the dolls' house – red lobsters, ham, fish, a dessert, some pears, and oranges. Beatrix identified with Timmy Willie, a country mouse. Faced with eight courses at Johnny Town-mouse's dinner party, he pines for simple country food.

TIMMY WILLIE TREATS JOHNNY TOWN-MOUSE TO HERB "PUDDING"

PTOLEMY TORTOISE'S INVITATION TO MR. JEREMY FISHER

Mr. Jeremy Fisher. Pond House.

Mr. Alderman Ptolemy Tortoise

Requests the pleasure of
Mr. Jeremy Fisher's
Company at Dinner
on Dec. 25th

(there will be a snail)   R.S.V.P.

INVITATIONS

In Beatrix Potter's society all parties began with a formal, written invitation. Her characters often send invitations, in the tales and in miniature letters to children (such as the two printed here). People like Tabitha Twitchit are always jealous of invitations to others, especially to a social inferior like Duchess. No one likes to be left out.

MR. JEREMY FISHER ACCEPTS HIS INVITATION

Mr. Alderman Ptolemy Tortoise
Melon Pit,
South Border.

Mr. Jeremy Fisher accepts with pleasure Alderman P. Tortoise's kind invitation to dinner for Dec. 25.

Guests at a 19th-century dinner party raised a toast to the lady of the house to thank her for her hospitality. Beatrix Potter's characters are (with one or two exceptions) equally polite.

Even Mr. Jackson, an uninvited guest, has the good manners to raise a toast. "Tiddly, widdly, widdly! Your very good health, Mrs. Tittlemouse!"

BAD MANNERS

Mr. Jackson the toad visits Mrs. Tittlemouse uninvited, drips water onto her floors, and refuses to eat anything but honey. No wonder she doesn't invite him in for her spring cleaning party. Instead she and her friends pass him acorn-cups of honey-dew through the window.

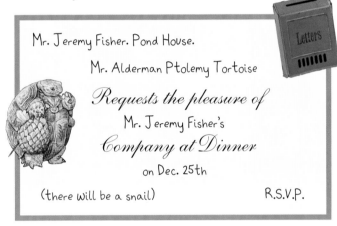

A FIERCE BAD RABBIT (RIGHT) NEVER SAYS "PLEASE"

MR. JEREMY FISHER

MR. JEREMY FISHER WEARS the clothes of a gentleman and reads a newspaper, but he is a thoroughly froggy frog. Being amphibian, he lives in a little damp house among the buttercups at the edge of a pond. He is an avid fisherman, though not always a very successful one. When he sees large drops of rain splashing on the pond, he puts on his mackintosh (raincoat) and galoshes and sets off with enormous hops to his boat.

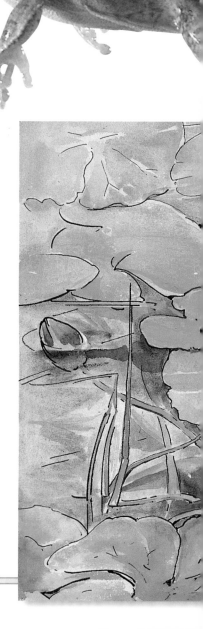

A SCOTTISH STORY

Mr. Jeremy Fisher's adventures were first described in a picture letter to Eric Moore in 1893. (Beatrix Potter had sent another letter to his brother Noel the day before, about Peter Rabbit.) In this version, Mr. Jeremy Fisher lived by a river, not a pond, and went fishing in a wooden boat instead of a lily pad. His river was very much like the Tay, in Scotland, where Beatrix and her family rented a house for the summer. And his boat was very much like the rowing boat her father used.

Rupert Potter took this photograph of the Tay River (above). Like Mr. Jeremy Fisher, he was a gentleman and an avid fisherman.

ERIC MOORE

The opening scene of Beatrix Potter's 1894 story, A Frog he would a-fishing go (left), shows that a true fisherman always checks the weather.

FROGS OUT OF FAVOR

In 1894, Beatrix sent Ernest Nister, a printer, 10 drawings for a new story, *A Frog he would a-fishing go.* This frog has no name but is just like Jeremy. Nister offered her less money than expected, "as people do not want frogs now." She stood her ground, and Nister bought nine of the drawings for a children's annual.

MR. JEREMY FISHER IN BRONZE, WITH A FINE FISH ON HIS LINE

Beatrix retold her Frog-a-fishing story in 1895, in a letter with pictures for her young cousin Molly Gaddum (above).

FISHING IN THE LAKE DISTRICT

Mr. Jeremy Fisher popped up again when Beatrix got to know the Lake District. In 1905 she sent a manscript to her editor, Norman Warne. "I'm afraid you don't like *frogs* but it would make pretty pictures with water-forget-me-nots, lilies, etc." He agreed, and published *The Tale of Mr. Jeremy Fisher* in 1906. By now the frog had moved from a river to a lake – Esthwaite Water, perhaps, or Moss Eccles Tarn, not far from Sawrey where Beatrix used to stay.

MOSS ECCLES TARN (LEFT), WHERE BEATRIX PLANTED SOME WATER LILIES

A fishing party at Windermere (right) shows off its salmon catch for Rupert Potter's camera. Beatrix and Bertram are sitting in the back of the boat.

To catch a dish of minnows for his dinner, Mr. Jeremy Fisher takes his rod and his basket to the pond, and pushes out his boat with a reed pole. His boat is round and green, and very like the other lily leaves.

When Mr. Jeremy Fisher hooks, then loses a stickleback, the other little fishes put their heads out and laugh at him. But something much worse is lurking below...

Beatrix sketched water lilies (left) at Esthwaite Water in 1906.

Mr. Jeremy Fisher comes home with no rod, basket, or galoshes, and no fish. Undaunted, he changes for dinner, invites his friends around, and serves roasted grasshopper with ladybug sauce.

FROGS IN TRANSIT

Frogs and Beatrix were old friends. Her journal for 1884 records, "Poor little *Punch* died on the 11th., green frog, had him five or six years. He has been on extensive journeys." Twenty years on, Warne thought Mr. Jeremy Fisher should be green. Beatrix brought an ordinary common frog into their office to prove he should be brown. This little fisherman went on to be one of her best-loved characters.

PAGEFUL OF FROGS

TOM KITTEN

THREE LITTLE KITTENS CALLED Mittens, Tom Kitten, and Moppet are in trouble. Their mother, Mrs. Tabitha Twitchit, is expecting friends for tea. She calls the kittens indoors to wash them and dress them in all kinds of elegant uncomfortable clothes. Then, unwisely, she turns them out into the garden and tells them to keep their clothes clean by walking on their hind legs and keeping away from the Puddle-ducks. Readers know she will be disappointed.

TOM KITTEN'S HOME

Beatrix Potter knew Tom Kitten's home inside and out – it was Hill Top, the farmhouse she bought in the Lake District village of Near Sawrey in 1905. At the beginning of *The Tale of Tom Kitten*, Mrs. Tabitha Twitchit brings her three kittens up the garden path, past a trellis covered with roses, toward the front porch. Beyond is the gate to the farmyard. This is the path Beatrix took to go in and out of Hill Top. She planted the borders on either side. Visitors take the same path today.

MRS. TABITHA TWITCHIT BRINGS HER THREE LITTLE KITTENS INDOORS

Buckle Yeat (left) is just down the road from Tom Kitten and Beatrix Potter's home. She sketched it in 1907 for her new story.

Three Puddle-ducks march along the road – pit pat paddle pat! pit pat waddle pat! They stop by the kittens' wall and try on their discarded clothes.

TOM KITTEN'S VILLAGE

When the kittens are sent out to play, they jump onto the wall at the bottom of the garden. From here they can see along the village street and over houses and fields to the hills beyond. Sawrey cottages and gardens had already featured in *The Pie and the Patty-Pan*. In 1907 Beatrix sketched more of the views she knew and loved, as settings for her next three books.

Hill Top's garden (left) was laid out by Beatrix in 1906, and planted with cottage blooms from her neighbors. The pink rose she put in still clambers over the porch.

Dressed in their ill-fitting finery, the Puddle-ducks set off up the road – pit pat, paddle pat! pit pat, waddle pat! They end up in a pond.

The Puddle-ducks' route (left) is based on a sketch of Stoney Lane (above). Stoney Lane starts across the road from Hill Top and winds up the hill.

A PERFECT PICKLE

Beatrix borrowed the name for Mrs. Tabitha Twitchit from the farm cat she met while renovating Hill Top. For Tom Kitten, she used the same model as for Miss Moppet (see page 92). It was "very young and a most fearful pickle." When *The Tale of Tom Kitten* was ready, she dedicated it "to all Pickles – especially to those that get upon my garden wall."

BEATRIX POTTER PHOTOGRAPHED ON HER FRONT PORCH AT HILL TOP, 1913

TOM KITTEN WRITES TO DREW FAYLE

Master D. Fayle
Kylemore

Dear Master Fayle
   I wish you a Happy New Year rather late! Miss Potter did have to write such a lot of letters. Do you know she gets letters from little girls as far off as New Zealand? and America & Russia. And now somebody wants to give her a Norway kitten! I rather am afraid I shall fight it!
   yr aff friend
   Tom Kitten.

SKETCH OF A CAT'S FACE

MORE DUCKS

Beatrix had to return to London for the winter and finished her sketches there. For the last picture in the book, she found some dabbling ducks in Putney Park. Beatrix called the three Puddle-ducks Mr. Drake, Rebeccah, and Jemima. Jemima was named after a duck at Hill Top. She was about to star in a book of her own.

PUDDLE-DUCK SOAP DISH

JEMIMA PUDDLE-DUCK

ON THE OTHER SIDE of Tom Kitten's house is the farmyard, where many other animals live – hens, cows, Kep the collie-dog, and the family of Puddle-ducks. Jemima Puddle-duck makes a bid for independence and decides to build her nest in the woods, over the hill and far away from the farm. However, the handsome foxy-whiskered gentleman who offers to assist her is not as well-meaning as he seems.

DINNER PLACE CARDS INSCRIBED "WHOSE IS THIS?" AND "HERE'S THE PLACE FOR ME!"

A FARMYARD TALE

In 1908, Beatrix Potter dedicated a new story to the Cannon children as "A Farmyard Tale for Ralph and Betsy." Their parents managed Hill Top Farm for Beatrix. Mrs. Cannon appears in the first picture as the farmer's wife who won't let Jemima hatch her eggs. Ralph and Betsy find some of the eggs in a rhubarb patch.

Jemima tries all kinds of hiding places for her eggs, even the rhubarb patch. But they are always found and taken away. She needs a more secluded spot.

SKETCH OF DUCKS AND HENS AT HILL TOP FARM

BEATRIX POTTER'S DUCKLINGS

JEMIMA DOLL MADE BY FARNELL & CO., 1909

BEATRIX POTTER'S DUCKS

Jemima was the name of one of the ducks at Hill Top, and of many ducks to come. In 1933, Beatrix would write to a friend, "You ask after cross Mrs P. Duck; she sat and she sat, and when I (at great peril) lifted her off her nest in the hay barn, she was sitting on nothing. There had been an egg; whether she had eaten it, or Samuel Whiskers – [I] cannot say! The previous summer she hatched out one black chicken!"

THE FOXY GENTLEMAN

In the woods, Jemima meets an elegantly dressed gentleman sitting on a tree stump among the foxgloves. She has no idea he is a villain, but Beatrix did. Long before she became a farmer, she had illustrated foxes of great greed and cunning from Aesop's fables and Brer Rabbit stories. Jemima's fox addresses her as "Madam." However, after he sends her off to find onions and herbs, Beatrix shows him in his true colors – on all fours, without his elegant clothes, admiring her nine eggs.

The hospitable gentleman shows Jemima into his summer residence and invites her to make a nest there. She is surprised to find it full of feathers.

Kep the collie forms a rescue party at the Tower Bank Arms (right), which is next door to Hill Top.

UNFINISHED STUDY OF
FOXGLOVES

Beatrix Potter's collie Kep (right) stood guard over her sheep in the heavy snow of March 1909.

A DOG CALLED KEP

Back at the farm, Jemima meets the collie-dog Kep, who asks her where she has been. When she describes her foxy gentleman, Kep knows exactly who he is, and rounds up two foxhound puppies to deal with him. Thanks to Kep's quick thinking, Jemima survives to lay more eggs. Four of them hatch into ducklings.

BEATRIX AND KEP AT HILL TOP,
PHOTOGRAPHED IN 1913

SAMUEL WHISKERS

UNBEKNOWNST TO TABITHA TWITCHIT and her three kittens, there is someone else living secretly in their house. So Tom Kitten lands himself in more trouble than he bargains for when he hides from his mother in the big chimney at Hill Top. He loses his way in a a maze of little passages in the old house. Finally he comes face to face with two strangers in a hideout under the attic floor, the rat Samuel Whiskers and his wife Anna Maria.

In a picture letter to Winifred Warne in 1908, Beatrix showed Anna Maria and Samuel Whiskers redecorating with her wallpaper.

A FUNNY OLD HOUSE

Beatrix Potter explored her new house at Hill Top from top to bottom (including the attic) and described it in letters to Millie, Norman Warne's sister. "I never saw such a place for hide & seek, & funny cupboards & closets." Tom Kitten's hiding place is the chimney above the old-fashioned stove in Beatrix Potter's front kitchen.

Tom Kitten makes up his mind to climb right to the top of the chimney and on to the roof to catch sparrows. He soon looks like a sooty little chimney sweep.

"IT REQUIRES DOUGH AND A PAT OF BUTTER, AND A ROLLING-PIN"

SAMUEL WHISKERS
KNITTED DOLL

Roly-poly pudding requires dough, a pat of butter and a rolling pin from the kitchen. Samuel Whiskers boldly uses the front staircase.

When Tom Kitten strays into the rats' attic, Anna Maria ties him up with string and Samuel Whiskers tells her to make a kitten dumpling roly-poly pudding for his dinner.

WATCH OUT FOR THIEVES

When Beatrix Potter bought Hill Top, the resident rats saw no need to move out. "Mrs Cannon has seen a rat sitting up eating its dinner under the kitchen table in the middle of the afternoon," she told Millie Warne. Despite her best efforts to make the house rat-proof, they were still there two years later. Beatrix noticed they were stealing strips of wallpaper that lined a large closet – "rather a pretty green & gold paper."

BEATRIX POTTER'S
FAMILY CREST (ABOVE),
AT HILL TOP

A RAT CALLED SAMMY

Beatrix Potter dedicated her new book to a childhood pet: "In Remembrance of 'SAMMY,' The intelligent pink-eyed Representative of a Persecuted (but Irrepressible) Race An affectionate little Friend, and most accomplished Thief!" Many years later Beatrix remembered her aunt, "a stout elderly lady who did not altogether appreciate his friendly advances," giving Sammy a hard-boiled egg and watching him roll it along a passage to his box.

Beatrix Potter gave Samuel Whiskers his own coat of arms in a bookplate inside the front cover of his book. His motto is "Resurgam!!!," Latin for "I shall triumph again."

A Frog He Would A-Wooing Go (*above*) *by Randolph Caldecott, 1883, clearly influenced Beatrix Potter's Mr. Jeremy Fisher, and probably her portly Samuel Whiskers and skinny Anna Maria too.*

LAKE DISTRICT FARMYARD – IS THIS SAMUEL WHISKERS AND ANNA MARIA'S NEW HOME?

Samuel Whiskers and Anna Maria hear Tom Kitten's rescuers and depart at once to Farmer Potatoes' barn. Beatrix sees them flee with their bundles – on her wheelbarrow.

"Farmer Potatoes" (right) and his daughters Ruth and Mary Postlethwaite lived up the road from Hill Top, in Smithy Lane.

GONE BUT NOT FORGOTTEN

"We are discovered and interrupted, Anna Maria; let us collect our property – and other people's – and depart at once." Samuel Whiskers was gone (for now) but his name lived on when his book came out in 1908. One young fan, the son of Beatrix Potter's cousin Caroline Hutton, wrote to Beatrix from Scotland: "We have Samuele Whiskers all over the house: he ran over my hanktuhes in the laundrey one day, and made them very dirty."

FARMER POTATOES WRITES TO SAMUEL WHISKERS

To Samuel Rat,
High Barn

Sir,
I hereby give you one day's notice to quit my barn & stables and byre, with your wife, children, grandchildren & great grandchildren to the latest generation.

signed: William Potatoes,
farmer

witness: Gilbert Cat
& John Stoat-Ferret

A Funny Old House

Beatrix Potter had owned Hill Top for about a year when she started writing *The Tale of Tom Kitten*. She included her favorite views of her new home, looking almost exactly as they do today, in the tales of Tom Kitten, Jemima Puddle-duck, Samuel Whiskers, and (a few years later) Pigling Bland. In 1947 the National Trust opened the house to the public. "It is indeed a funny old house," Beatrix once said; "it would amuse children very much."

The front door at Hill Top appears in The Tale of Samuel Whiskers.

The fire in the front kitchen (right) was a cosy spot for sitting with friends.

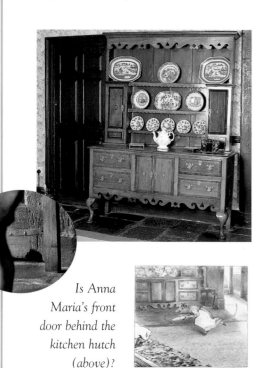

Is Anna Maria's front door behind the kitchen hutch (above)?

At the top of the stairs (below), Samuel Whiskers pushes along the rolling pin he has stolen from the kitchen.

Halfway up the front stairs (left) Tabitha Twitchit calls Tom Kitten, who is hiding.

Tom Kitten is hiding in the chimney that goes up from the kitchen fireplace. If he climbed right to the top and out onto the rooftop, he would have a wonderful view of the village of Near Sawrey (right) and the little lane that winds over the hill beyond.

INTO THE GARDEN

WHEN BEATRIX POTTER FIRST bought Hill Top, the garden was "very overgrown & untidy." Within a year she had new paths and flowerbeds, planted with "something out of nearly every garden in the village." She also restocked her farmyard next door, with 16 new ewes joining her two pigs, six cows, Puddle-ducks, and hens.

Tabitha Twitchit brings her kittens up the garden path which Beatrix designed and had built. Visitors to Hill Top still use this path today.

Beatrix planted the old pink rose that still scrambles over Tabitha Twitchit's porch. The porch is made from two slabs of local stone topped with slate.

Opposite the porch is a vegetable plot. The rhubarb patch (above) looks like a good hiding place for Jemima Puddle-duck's eggs, if only it weren't so close to the house.

At the bottom of the path, a wooden gate (left) opens onto the main road through the village. Pickles who get up onto the garden wall can see everyone who passes by.

In the winter, Hill Top's sheep come in to the farmyard (above) for food and shelter. Kep the collie-dog lives there too. In spring, Jemima Puddle-duck raises her yellow ducklings in the farmyard, safe from any foxy gentlemen living in the woods nearby.

THE FLOPSY BUNNIES

BEATRIX POTTER FANS WANTED to know more about Peter Rabbit and Benjamin Bunny. In 1909 she wrote a new story, dedicated to "all little friends of Mr. McGregor and Peter and Benjamin." Time has passed, both rabbits are now grown up, and Benjamin has married Peter's sister Flopsy. Peter grows his own vegetables, but the feud with Mr. McGregor continues. Things look bad when the gardener captures Benjamin's six little children, the Flopsy Bunnies.

SOPORIFIC LETTUCES

"It is said that the effect of eating too much lettuce is 'soporific.'" So begins Beatrix Potter's 14th tale. Warne thought children might not understand the word "soporific." So she went on to explain, "*I* have have never felt sleepy after eating lettuces; but then *I* am not a rabbit." Readers know they are in for a treat.

LETTUCE AND GUINEA PIGS BY BRITISH ARTIST EDWARD LEAR (1812–1888)

If there isn't enough to eat, and Peter has no cabbages to spare, the Flopsy Bunnies head for the rubbish heap outside Mr. McGregor's garden. One day – oh joy! – they find a quantity of lettuces there.

LETHAL LETTUCES

The picture of the Flopsies asleep under a lettuce may pay homage to an artist and humorist Beatrix admired, Edward Lear. In his *History of the Seven Families of Lake Pipple-Popple*, seven greedy guinea pigs lay in a similar pose. In their haste to feed, they bumped their noses on a lettuce and fell down dead.

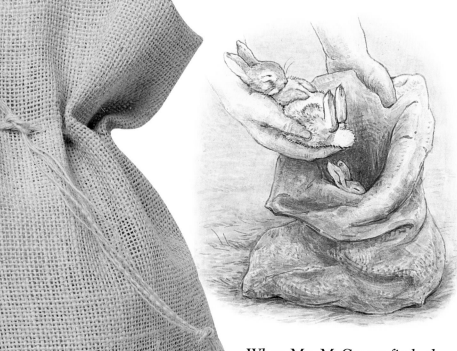

When Mr. McGregor finds the "six leetle rabbits" he puts them (still asleep) into a sack and ties it up. But while he is putting away the mowing machine a mouse comes to the rescue.

SIX LEETLE RABBITS WRITE TO LITTLE JOHN HOUGH

Dear Master John Hough
  I wish you a Merry Christmas! I am going to have an apple for my Christmas dinner & some celery tops. The cabbages are all frosted, but there is lots of hay.
  yrs aff
First Flopsy Bunny.
  ✕ ✕ ✕ ✕ ✕ ✕

MR. McGregor's New Garden

In *The Tale of Benjamin Bunny*, Mr. McGregor's garden was at Fawe Park in the Lake District. For her new book Beatrix Potter moved him to Gwaenynog, near Denbigh in North Wales. Gwaenynog was her uncle's house, and Beatrix often stayed there. She described its large walled garden as "the prettiest kind of garden, where bright old-fashioned flowers grow amongst the currant bushes."

Beatrix stayed at Gwaenynog (above) in March 1909, while working on The Tale of the Flopsy Bunnies.

Mr. McGregor carries his sack of rabbits (or so he thinks) home to Mrs. McGregor. The Flopsies follow at a safe distance, to see what happens next.

GWAENYNOG SKETCH (RIGHT)
FOR MR. McGregor's
GARDEN PATH (ABOVE)

Dear Master John,
  I wish you the same as my oldest brother, and I am going to have the same dinner
    yrs aff
  2nd Flopsy Bunny
  X X X X X X X

Dear Master John
I have not learned to rite prop perly.
  Love from
4th (Miss) F Bunny
  X X

Dear Master John
  X X X X
  X X X
5th Miss F. Bunny

Dear Master Hough,
  I wish you the compliments of the season. We have got new fur tippets for Christmas.
    yrs aff
  3rd (Miss) F. Bunny
  X X X

THE SMALLEST TWO
FLOPSIES CAN ONLY
SCRIBBLE KISSES (RIGHT)

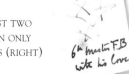

  X
  X X
  X X
6th Master F. B.
  with his love.

77

MRS. TITTLEMOUSE

THE UNLIKELY HEROINE WHO comes to the rescue
of the Flopsy Bunnies is the tiny wood mouse,
Mrs. Thomasina Tittlemouse. *The Tale of Mrs.
Tittlemouse* takes us into her tiny home in a bank
under a hedge. She has yards and yards of sandy
passages leading to storerooms and cellars, and a surprising
number of uninvited guests. Beatrix Potter was sympathetic –
she had similar problems with Samuel Whiskers and several
other uninvited guests in her farmhouse at Hill Top.

ALWAYS SWEEPING

Mrs. Tittlemouse was a most terribly
tidy particular little mouse, always
sweeping and dusting the soft sandy
floors. In the days before vacuum
cleaners, housework was hard work.
But Beatrix probably knew many others
just as particular as Thomasina – her
mother or her mother's housekeeper
perhaps, or her neighbors in Sawrey.

*Mrs. Tittlemouse has already seen
a beetle, a ladybug, and a spider
in her house. When she finds
some bees and their nest of untidy
dry moss, she gets annoyed. "I am
not in the habit of letting lodgings;
this is an intrusion!"*

STUDY OF A WOOD
MOUSE, 1886

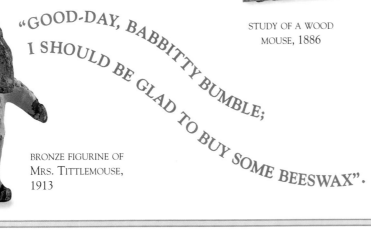

"GOOD-DAY, BABBITTY BUMBLE;
I SHOULD BE GLAD TO BUY SOME BEESWAX".

BRONZE FIGURINE OF
MRS. TITTLEMOUSE,
1913

CREEPY-CRAWLIES

Since childhood, Beatrix had studied and sketched
insects and other creepy-crawlies. Warne wasn't sure her
readers would like them as much as she did. So out went
the earwig Mrs. Tittlemouse first found, and in came a
beetle. Wood lice became "three creepy-crawly people."
And a centipede behind the soup
tureen was replaced by a butterfly
on the sugar bowl.

A RUNAWAY TOAD

In 1894, the Potters rented a house for the summer which was "not over clean" and had bugs in the back passage. Beatrix was more upset by the loss of her toad, who jumped off a windowsill. "I had had him more than a year and very tame, turning sharply round for food when I put my hand near him."

Mr. Jackson, also uninvited, sits and smiles in front of Mrs. Tittlemouse's fire, and drips water off his coat tails. After he helps her with the bees, the untidiness is something dreadful.

Beatrix drew The Toads' Tea Party *(above) for a book of rhymes in 1905. Mrs. Tittlemouse also has a party, when her house is all beautifully neat and clean – Mr. Jackson is not invited.*

Beatrix sketched bees and other flying insects for her own interest c. 1895 (top), and years later these ladybugs and spiders for The Tale of Mrs. Tittlemouse.

"NOW WHAT I REALLY–REALLY SHOULD LIKE – WOULD BE A LITTLE DISH OF HONEY!"

Mrs. Tittlemouse begins her spring cleaning, which lasts for two weeks.

The Tale of Mrs. Tittlemouse *was first written out as a New Year's present for Nellie Warne (above). Her family called it "Nellie's little book."*

NELLIE'S LITTLE BOOK

Beatrix dedicated her new book to Nellie Warne, Harold's daughter. When Warne printed it and sent Beatrix her first copies, she told them, "The buff copy is the prettiest color, though it may not keep so clean. I think it should prove popular with little girls." Mrs. Tittlemouse would have kept her copy away from Mr. Jackson, who never wipes his feet and leaves large wet footprints everywhere.

GINGER AND PICKLES

THE MOST POPULAR SHOP in Peter Rabbit's village is run by Ginger the cat and Pickles the terrier. Everyone shops there, from Peter Rabbit and Mrs. Tiggy-winkle to Samuel Whiskers and Mr. Jeremy Fisher. But the customers are reluctant to pay for what they buy, which finally spells ruin for the shop's owners.

FIRST EDITION OF *THE TALE OF GINGER AND PICKLES*, 1909

JOHN DORMOUSE (ABOVE, IN BED), WITH DISSATISFIED CUSTOMERS

THE VILLAGE SHOP

Ginger and Pickles' shop is based on the village shop in Sawrey, which was owned by the local blacksmith, John Taylor. Beatrix said the new tale was a big hit with her neighbors: "it has got a good many views which can be recognized in the village which is what they like, they are all quite jealous of each others [sic] houses and cats getting into a book."

The customers come in crowds and buy 10 times more at Ginger and Pickles' than at Tabitha Twitchit's. But they never pay.

POLICEMAN DOLL (RIGHT), MADE BY STEIFF IN GERMANY

A DORMOUSE

John Taylor wanted to be in the new book. Beatrix knew his wife and daughter ran the shop while he stayed in bed. "So I said how could I draw him if he would not get up? and he considered for several days, and then 'sent his respects, and thinks he might pass as a dormouse!'" And so he did, as John Dormouse.

CANDLE FOR MICE, FROM JOHN DORMOUSE

UNLIMITED CREDIT

In the days before cars, cash machines, and credit cards, people shopped locally, knew their shopkeeper, and often bought on account. Instead of paying on the spot, they were sent a bill at the end of the month. Even then they might be slow to pay.

LUCINDA DOLL WRITES TO GINGER AND PICKLES

Beatrix sketched John Taylor's shop (above) as a background for Ginger and Pickles'.

SOAP FOR MRS. TIGGY-WINKLE

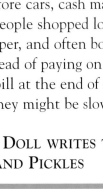

Miss Lucinda Doll has received Messrs Pickle & Ginger's account, about which there is some mistake. She has lived for some months upon German plaster provisions & saw dust, and had given no order for the groceries mentioned in the bill.

Miss Lucinda Doll,
Doll's House

Ginger and Pickles find a policeman doll on the premises and fear a court summons, for they have no money for a dog license and taxes. They close the shop and run away.

When Ginger and Pickles close, and then John Dormouse, their customers go to Sally Henny Penny. She insists on cash.

There is "something to please everybody" in a miniature Ginger and Pickles shop (below), but the cash register is still empty.

OPEN FOR BUSINESS

Beatrix Potter knew villagers relied on their shop to stock what they needed and at affordable prices. When Ginger and Pickles close, rival Tabitha Twitchit tries to take advantage of her monopoly by raising her prices. John Dormouse sells only peppermints and substandard candles. But Sally Henny Penny offers "a remarkable assortment of bargains" and "something to please everybody."

HADDOCK FOR GINGER

SNUFF FOR
SAMUEL
WHISKERS

PEPPERMINTS

RED SPOTTED HANKIES
FOR PETER RABBIT

KNITTED PICKLES
DOLL WITH APRON
AND ORDER BOOK

SHINY NEW
GALOSHES FOR
MR. JEREMY FISHER

TIMMY TIPTOES

IN 1911 THE ANIMAL CHARACTERS in the woods near Hill Top were joined by some new arrivals. *The Tale of Timmy Tiptoes* features gray squirrels, chipmunks, and a black bear, which were all American animals. The Peter Rabbit Books now had so many fans in the United States that Beatrix Potter wanted to write a story that would appeal especially to those readers.

WANTED: ONE BLACK BEAR

Beatrix needed models for her new characters. She read an illustrated guide to American animals. One of her cousins lent her a pet chipmunk. And she visited a black bear at the Zoological Gardens (now London Zoo) in Regent's Park. In her illustrations for *Timmy Tiptoes*, they all live in the woods around Hill Top, her home in the Lake District.

SKETCHES OF A BLACK BEAR (ABOVE) AND A CHIPMUNK (RIGHT)

Ten years after Beatrix saw her bear at the zoo, Christopher Milne met a bear there named Winnie. His father wrote Winnie-the-Pooh *(1926).*

Timmy and his wife Goody hide their nuts in a tree hole that had belonged to a woodpecker. But the other squirrels think Timmy has stolen their nuts, and push him into the hole too.

Inside the tree hole, a chipmunk called Chippy Hackee kindly lends Timmy his nightcap and feeds him quantities of nuts. Timmy gets fatter and fatter.

A FALL TALE

Beatrix knew all about squirrels gathering nuts at the end of summer, and storing them for winter when food is scarce. *The Tale of Squirrel Nutkin* started with a similar search. Chipmunks also hoard nuts. At the end of *The Tale of Timmy Tiptoes*, Beatrix hints that it is Chippy Hackee, not Timmy Tiptoes, who has been stealing the other squirrels' supplies.

LONDON'S ZOOLOGICAL GARDENS (ABOVE), C. 1890s

TIMMY TIPTOES IS A GRAY SQUIRREL

SQUIRREL NUTKIN IS A RED SQUIRREL

In Beatrix Potter's day, red squirrels abounded. In the 1920s, however, gray squirrels introduced from America took over their habitat. Britain now has far more Timmy Tiptoes than Nutkins – but no chipmunks or bears.

PETER RABBIT IN THE US

The Peter Rabbit books had been popular in the United States from the start, when Henry Altemus of Philadelphia published *The Tale of Peter Rabbit* – without Warne's permission. Warne soon established its copyright by bringing out its own American edition. That didn't stop other pirates, in the United States and elsewhere. So fans now looked for the original and authorized editions.

EARLY PIRATE EDITIONS OF *PETER RABBIT* (LEFT), WITH NEW ILLUSTRATIONS AND STORIES

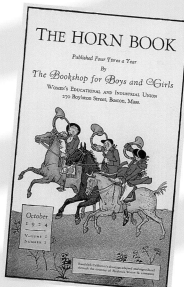

THE HORN BOOK

Published Four Times a Year

By

The Bookshop for Boys and Girls

WOMEN'S EDUCATIONAL AND INDUSTRIAL UNION
270 Boylston Street, Boston, Mass.

October 1924
VOLUME I NUMBER I

THE HORN BOOK MAGAZINE'S FIRST ISSUE, 1924

MOST WELCOME!

Some of Beatrix Potter's American fans visited her in the Lake District and became her friends. "Most welcome!" she told Helen Dean Fish, an editor from New York. "I always tell nice Americans to send other nice Americans along ... You come because you understand the books, and love the same old tales that I do – not from any impertinent curiosity. [P.S.] Come up early afternoon and stay for tea."

SPREADING THE WORD

The first American to visit Beatrix was Anne Carroll Moore of the New York Public Library, in 1921. Another promoter of children's books was Bertha Mahony Miller, founder and editor of *The Horn Book Magazine* in Boston. She never met Beatrix, but she published major articles on her work, inspiration, and concern for the English countryside.

POSTER C. 1910 FOR ONE OF THE TRANS-ATLANTIC LINERS THAT BROUGHT FANS AND FAN MAIL

BERTHA MAHONY MILLER, 1929

HORN BOOK CARAVAN, ON ITS FIRST ROAD SHOW IN 1920

MR. TOD

IN *THE TALE OF MR. TOD* Beatrix Potter claimed to be tired of writing books about "well-behaved people" – instead she wanted to make a story about "two disagreeable people." Mr. Tod the fox and Tommy Brock the badger are indeed disagreeable, but fortunately they spend so much time being unpleasant to each other that they prove no match for our heroes Peter Rabbit and Benjamin Bunny.

PETER RABBIT TO THE RESCUE

Benjamin Bunny once helped Peter get his coat back from Mr. McGregor. Now Peter helps his cousin rescue his six little children – facing not only the badger who's kidnapped them but a fox as well. No wonder the British novelist Graham Greene (1904–1991) would later compare the "epic personalities" of Peter and Benjamin to another heroic duo, Don Quixote and Sancho Panza.

Tommy Brock does occasionally eat rabbit pie, when other food is really scarce. He kidnaps the six little Flopsy Bunnies and carries them off in a sack.

Beatrix Potter's 1907 sketchbook (below) includes a drawing of what looks like Mr. Tod's house.

The smell of badger is unmistakable, so Benjamin Bunny and Peter Rabbit track Tommy Brock all the way to Mr. Tod's house. Enter Mr. Tod...

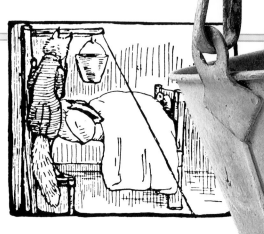

OUTRAGED TO FIND TOMMY BROCK IN HIS BED, MR. TOD SETS A TRAP WITH A PAIL OF WATER

MR. TOD THINKS TOMMY BROCK IS ASLEEP WHILE HE TIES THE ROPE AROUND A TREE OUTSIDE

MR. TOD TIED THE KNOT SO TIGHT HE HAS TO GNAW THROUGH THE ROPE TO RELEASE THE PAIL

NOT A SOUND – THE PAIL MUST HAVE HIT POOR OLD TOMMY BROCK AND KILLED HIM DEAD!

A TERRIFIC BATTLE

The Tale of Mr. Tod was published in 1912. In 1913, six-year-old Harold Botcherby of London wondered how the "terrific battle" between Mr. Tod and Tommy Brock had ended. Beatrix Potter wrote back, "My dear Harold, I have inquired about Mr. Tod & Tommy Brock, & I am sorry to tell you they are still quarrelling."

BEATRIX POTTER'S
SKETCH OF ESTHWAITE
WATER (RIGHT), 1909

While Tommy Brock grapples with Mr. Tod, Peter and Benjamin rescue the Flopsy Bunnies from Mr. Tod's oven.

COUNTRYSIDE IN MINIATURE

"Tod" and "Brock" are the old country names for fox and badger. Beatrix Potter's Tod and Brock live "at the top of Bull Banks, under Oatmeal Crag," which rise gently behind the village of Sawrey and overlook Esthwaite Water. *The Tale of Mr. Tod* is one of her longer stories, with 15 watercolors and 42 line drawings in the style of old English woodcuts. Many are masterpieces of landscape in miniature.

ESTHWAITE WATER (ABOVE)

UNCLE REMUS

Beatrix knew of another battle of wits, between Brer Rabbit and Brer Fox in Joel Chandler Harris's *Uncle Remus* stories of the 1880s. For her own amusement, Beatrix had reillustrated scenes from these American classics, where Brer Fox or Brer Rabbit pretend to be dead, and Brer Rabbit rescues a terrapin hanging in a sack in Brer Fox's kitchen.

Beatrix Potter's Uncle Remus *(right), 1893. "Mighty funny. Brer Fox look like he dead, yit he dont do like he dead."*

"TOMMY BROCK OPENED BOTH EYES, AND LOOKED AT THE ROPE AND GRINNED."

Over the Hills and Far Away

Beatrix Potter had a new life,
as wife, farmer, and conservationist.
The later tales reflect this change –
from Pigling Bland who leaves home
and meets his true love, to Little Pig
Robinson who escapes to a tropical
island in faraway seas.

CHANGING TIMES

IN 1913 BEATRIX POTTER got married, at the age of 47, to solicitor William Heelis. That year she also published a new book, *The Tale of Pigling Bland,* about a pig who finds love and dances "over the hills and far away." Pigling Bland's adventure (described overleaf) seemed to symbolize his author's escape into a new life. She now owned two farmhouses in the Lake District and on her marriage she and William moved into the larger one, Castle Cottage. As Mrs. Heelis, Beatrix was wife and farmer first, author second.

William Heelis's office in Hawkshead (above) is now open to the public as the National Trust's Beatrix Potter Gallery.

MICE DANCING, C. 1897 – WILLIAM LIKED DANCING TOO

A PROPOSAL, AND A SECRET

William Heelis was Beatrix Potter's solicitor in the Lake District, and had helped her find other pieces of land to add to Hill Top. She accepted his proposal gladly, but her parents were dismayed – until their son Bertram revealed that he had been secretly married for 11 years, happily and without inconveniencing his family. Beatrix and William's wedding went ahead.

BEATRIX AND WILLIAM'S ENGAGEMENT PHOTO

MORE DANCING (RIGHT), FROM AN 1890S CARD AND A SONG IN *THE SOLITARY MOUSE*, BOTH BY BEATRIX

"Pipe Wind! Dance Mouse
We'll have a wedding
In our own good house!"

A WEDDING PRESENT

After her wedding, Beatrix wrote to Millie Warne, Norman's sister and a close friend since his death. "I am sending you belated cake, which I hadn't the courage to do before!" In response to Millie's letter a few weeks later, she added, "Now if you want to get me a nice useful present that I shall always use & remember you by – get me Mrs. Beeton's cookery, please & write my name in it! Nothing like asking."

WILLIAM HEELIS, AN AVID SPORTSMAN, WITH BOWLING TROPHIES

Bertram, though married, still joined his family for the summer vacation in 1911 (below). Rupert Potter died at the age of 82 in 1914. In 1918, far more unexpectedly, Bertram died, aged just 46.

COOKING FOR WILLIAM

When *Mrs. Beeton's Book of Household Management* arrived, Beatrix wrote to Millie, "I do seem to have let you in for a large solid gift! I had no idea that Mrs Beeton had grown so stout. I shall be much amused to experiment with her; I already take exception to her direction to fry bacon in a cold pan. Wm. prefers blue smoke before the bacon is laid on the frying pan."

BEATRIX AND HER MOTHER AT CASTLE COTTAGE, SAWREY

MRS. BEETON'S BOOK OF HOUSEHOLD MANAGEMENT

VALENTINE'S CARD, WHICH STILL HANGS IN BEATRIX POTTER'S FARMHOUSE AT HILL TOP

WAR WORK

World War I broke out in 1914. As more and more working men enlisted, women took their place in factories and fields. In 1916, Louie Choyce wrote to Beatrix to offer help with the farm. Beatrix told her what to expect. "I have poultry, orchard, flower garden, vegetables, no glass [greenhouse], help with heavy digging, cooking ... and I single [pick] turnips when I can find time." "Choicey" stayed at Hill Top for the rest of the war, and became a lifelong friend.

LAND GIRLS IN WORLD WAR I (1914–1918)

PIGLING BLAND

BEATRIX GIVES PIGLING BLAND A LICENSE TO GO TO THE MARKET

BEATRIX POTTER HERSELF APPEARS at the start of this tale, trying to help the old mother pig Aunt Pettitoes control her unruly family of eight little piglets. The Tale follows the adventures of one of the piglets, Pigling Bland, as he leaves home to find his fortune at the market. He falls into the hands of the untrustworthy Mr. Piperson, but finally escapes "over the hills and far away" in the company of the charming little black girl-pig, Pig-wig.

Beatrix painted this little pig in a bath-time tub in 1899. The same pig reappeared in 1913 as Pigling Bland's sister Yock-yock.

A MODEL FOR PIG-WIG

"I have got two lovely pigs," Beatrix told Harold Warne's daughter Louie in 1907; "one is a little bigger than the other, she is very fat and black with a very turned up nose and the fattest cheeks I ever saw; she likes being tickled under the chin, she is a very friendly pig." But John Cannon, the farm manager at Hill Top, didn't want a black pig on the farm, so she became a pet for Beatrix.

BEATRIX POTTER'S SKETCHES OF PIG'S HEADS, C. 1910

Pigling Bland trots off to the market with his brother Alexander, a hopelessly volatile pig who loses his papers and goes back to Hill Top.

SAWREY CROSSROADS, WHERE PIGLING BLAND TAKES THE ROAD SIGNPOSTED "MARKET TOWN, 5 MILES" (HAWKSHEAD)

IN THE PIG PEN

By 1910 Beatrix had begun her story about her pigs. "I have done a little sketching when it does not rain," she told Millie Warne, "and I spent a very wet hour *inside* the pig stye drawing the pig. It tries to nibble my boots, which is interrupting." She dedicated her new Tale to Cecily and Charlie Townley, children of the farmer who had sold her the little black girl-pig.

NEW HORIZONS

"Market Town" is Hawkshead, where Beatrix went shopping. Local farmhouses, roads, and bridges that she knew appear in Pigling Bland's journey. Instead of Hawkshead, he and Pig-wig end up in Little Langdale, over the hills from Sawrey but not so very far away. Like Beatrix, they look forward to starting a new life.

Pigling Bland meets Pig-wig, a perfectly lovely little black Berkshire pig, and gives her his porridge. They agree to run away from Mr. Piperson, who is fattening them for bacon and ham.

The grocer that Pigling Bland and Pig-wig meet posed for this photo so Beatrix could copy his horse and cart for her new book.

LITTLE LANGDALE (LEFT), IN THE NEIGHBORING COUNTY OF WESTMORLAND

ARM IN ARM, PIGLING BLAND AND PIG-WIG WATCH THE SUN RISE OVER WESTMORLAND

"TOM, TOM, THE PIPER'S SON, STOLE A PIG AND AWAY HE RAN!"

HUMPBACKED STONE BRIDGE IN CUMBRIA, LIKE THE TWO IN THE TALE

ARM IN ARM

The book came out in 1913, the year Beatrix got married. She told a fan, "The portrait of two pigs arm in arm – looking at the sunrise – is not a portrait of me and Mr Heelis, though it is a view of where we used to walk on Sunday afternoons! When I want to put William in a book – it will have to be as some very tall thin animal."

91

A Fierce Bad Rabbit & Miss Moppet

As Beatrix Potter became more involved with farming, her books began to take second place in her life. But they were an established series now, with readers all over the world. Two of her books were simple tales for the very young – *The Story of A Fierce Bad Rabbit* and *The Story of Miss Moppet*. They were first published in 1906 as fold-out panoramas. But booksellers complained that they got unfolded in the shops. So Warne published them again in 1916, as little books in the Peter Rabbit series.

Harold Warne's daughters Louie (far left) and Nellie (left) were each given one of Beatrix Potter's manuscripts for her new stories.

FIRST EDITION OF *THE STORY OF A FIERCE BAD RABBIT*, 1906

A Really Naughty Rabbit

Everyone loved Peter Rabbit, but six-year-old Louie Warne thought he was too good. She wanted a story about a really naughty rabbit. So Beatrix wrote a new book for her. Peter had sneaked into Mr. McGregor's garden and lost his coat and shoes. The Fierce Bad Rabbit takes a carrot without saying "please" and (thanks to a man with a gun) ends up losing his carrot, tail, and whiskers. As both rabbits discover, crime doesn't pay.

Beatrix gave the original Fierce Bad Rabbit manuscript (above) to Louie Warne in February 1906. Louie's father Harold bound it in a wallet, in the same way the panorama was bound.

The Fierce Bad Rabbit takes a carrot from a nice gentle Rabbit, and scratches him very badly. Then there's a BANG!

PRETTY MISS MOPPET

Soon after Beatrix gave Louie Warne *A Fierce Bad Rabbit*, she began another panorama for babies, *The Story of Miss Moppet*. "I am trying to draw a kitten now, it is very pretty but such a dreadful little pickle; it is never still for a minute." In case her readers worried about Miss Moppet hurting the Mouse, Beatrix decided, "She should catch him by the tail / less unpleasant." The same kitten, borrowed from a man from Windermere who was working at Hill Top, also modeled for *The Tale of Tom Kitten*.

Miss Moppet catches the Mouse and ties him in a dust cloth. But the dust cloth has a hole, and the Mouse escapes.

FIRST EDITION OF *THE STORY OF MISS MOPPET*, 1906

That greedy old cat invites the rat to tea but doesn't leave him a single drop of milk.

THE SLY OLD CAT

Beatrix sketched out a third panorama, *The Sly Old Cat*, for Louie's sister Nellie. Warne wanted to publish it in 1907, so Beatrix borrowed Nellie's book to start new illustrations. But the first two panoramas did not sell well, and Warne cancelled the third one. In 1916, when *A Fierce Bad Rabbit* and *Miss Moppet* were turned into little books, Beatrix thought another artist could illustrate *The Sly Old Cat*. It didn't work out, and Nellie finally got her book back.

BEATRIX POTTER'S SKETCH OF A MOUSE TEACHING HER CHILDREN TO READ, C.1893

OLD EYES, NEW BOOKS

By 1916, Beatrix was approaching 50. She told her publisher, "You will have to get used to the idea that my eyes are giving way, whether you like it or not – and if I managed to do yet another book it would not be that cat story [*The Sly Old Cat*]." Instead of a new tale, though, she had in mind another book for the very young, this time a collection of nursery rhymes...

APPLEY DAPPLY & CECILY PARSLEY

BY 1917, BEATRIX POTTER was busier than ever, looking after her land and animals. Her publisher, however, was in financial difficulties and asked Beatrix if she would provide a new book. She had been collecting and illustrating nursery rhymes for many years and so she suggested she could put some of this material together and make a book. *Appley Dapply's Nursery Rhymes* begins with a little brown mouse who goes to the cupboard in somebody's house. She is especially fond of pies.

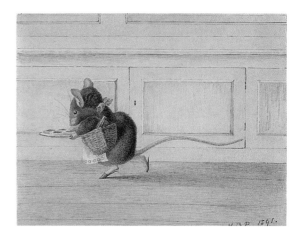

This picture for Appley Dapply with her pies was drawn in 1891, and redrawn for publication in 1917.

"THERE WAS A LADY LOVED A SWINE" (ABOVE), A RHYME IN WALTER CRANE'S *THE BABY'S OWN AESOP* (1887)

NURSERY FAVORITES

Beatrix had always loved traditional English nursery rhymes. Many of them had begun as adult ditties but were soon taken up by children, altered by them, and passed down from generation to generation. Popular collections published for children were illustrated by leading English artists such as Randolph Caldecott (1846–1886), Walter Crane (1845–1915), Kate Greenaway (1846–1901) – and now Beatrix Potter.

REDRAWN MR. PRICKLEPIN, USED IN 1917

Beatrix thought her original portrait of Old Mister Prickly Pin, for her 1905 Book of Rhymes, was one of her best. (It was modelled on a pet, Mrs. Tiggy's brother.)

You know the old woman who lived in a shoe? And had so many children She didn't know what to do?

I think if she lived in a little shoe-house – That little old woman was surely a mouse!

APPLEY DAPPLY'S OLD WOMAN IN A SHOE, IN RESIN (RIGHT), FIRST SKETCHED IN 1893

NEW BOOKS FROM OLD

In the 1890s, Beatrix had adapted and illustrated rhymes for two booklets, but didn't get them printed. In 1902, she had started sketching a book of animal rhymes, but Warne wanted more Tales instead. In 1917, the rhymes were finally published, with pictures drawn over three decades and in a great variety of styles.

In 1897, Cecily Parsley (right) made cider from apples. For Cecily Parsley's Nursery Rhymes in 1922, Warne said cowslips would be less intoxicating.

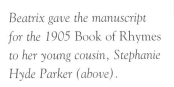

Beatrix gave the manuscript for the 1905 Book of Rhymes to her young cousin, Stephanie Hyde Parker (above).

RESIN FIGURINE OF CECILY PARSLEY RUNNING AWAY

CECILY PARSLEY'S BOOK

Appley Dapply's book was a success and Warne asked for another. Beatrix was reluctant. "People worry me for just one or two more books, but my eyes are getting weak, and I am tired of doing them." But by 1922 she "found time, somehow, to collect some old drawings and piece them together with some additions."

Beatrix dedicated Cecily Parsley's Nursery Rhymes to "Little Peter in New Zealand." Peter Tuckey was the nephew of one of her readers and had been orphaned in the war.

GUINEA PIGS GOING TO THEIR GARDEN, FIRST DRAWN IN 1893, REDRAWN IN 1922 (ABOVE)

TROUBLE AT WARNE

In 1917, Harold Warne was convicted of forging bills of exchange (checks) for £20,000, and sentenced to 18 months' hard labor. His brother Fruing took over the firm, and Beatrix did her best to help. "I hope Apply Dap will be in time to be useful." Early in 1918, she offered Warne another mouse story, The Tale of Johnny Town-Mouse.

JOHNNY TOWN-MOUSE

BEATRIX POTTER FOUND her town and country mice in an Aesop fable, but moved them from ancient Greece to the Lake District. Johnny lives in the town of Hawkshead, Timmy Willie in a Sawrey cottage garden. In spite of their mutual hospitality, neither mouse feels at ease in the other's territory and in the end they agree to differ. "One place suits one person, another place suits another person." Beatrix Potter's sympathies definitely lay with the country mouse.

The Country Mouse and The Town Mouse.

ANCIENT ANCESTORS

Aesop's fables are humorous satires dating back to the 6th century BC. They were among the first stories to be published for children, as education and entertainment. They feature animals that talk and behave like people, with all the human virtues and vices. Each fable ends with a proverb that sums up the moral of the story. Aesop's *Town Mouse and Country Mouse* concludes "Each to his own."

Timmy Willie goes to town by mistake in a hamper of vegetables after falling fast asleep among the peas. When the hamper is opened, out springs Timmy Willie, almost frightened to death.

The Tale of Johnny Town-Mouse came out in 1918, but Beatrix drew an earlier town and country mouse c. 1900 (right) and 1905 (above).

The Town Mouse and The Country Mouse.

GOOD MANNERS

Johnny Town-mouse introduces his unexpected guest with the utmost politeness to the other mice. They have long tails and white neckties and are too well bred to make personal remarks about Timmy Willie's more rustic appearance. Beatrix was brought up in equally refined society, and understood Timmy Willie's anxiety to "behave with company manners."

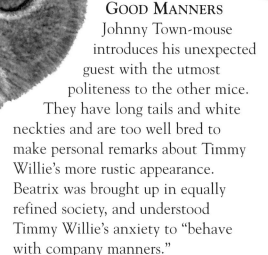

Timmy Willie crashes into the middle of a town-mouse dinner party. There are eight courses, with not much of anything, but truly elegant. A cat spoils Timmy Willie's appetite.

BEATRIX POTTER'S CLOGS, WHICH SHE WORE OUTDOORS ON THE FARM

HOME SICK

Timmy Willie cannot get used to life in the townhouse, with its noise, strange food, and resident cat. He longs to be back in his peaceful nest in a sunny bank, "warming his little fur coat and sniffing the smell of violets and spring grass." Beatrix too always longed to return from London to the countryside. But Johnny Town-mouse is baffled: "we have endeavoured to entertain you, Timothy William."

Timmy Willie misses his garden and the flowers – roses and pinks and pansies – and no noise except the birds and bees, and the lambs in the meadows.

Beatrix enjoyed sketching cows, but their mooing terrifies Johnny Town-mouse when he visits Timmy Willie in the country.

When Beatrix Potter's elderly mother left London in 1919 and came to live in the Lake District, she brought her city comforts with her – including a large car and staff.

LEAVING THE CITY

Johnny Town-mouse comes to stay with Timmy Willie, all spick and span and with a bag of golf clubs – the image of Dr. Parsons, William Heelis's golf partner. Timmy Willie offers him herb pudding and a bed of grass clippings, but Johnny Town-mouse finds the countryside a little damp and carries his tail over his arm, out of the mud. It's also too quiet – he doesn't stay long.

"For my part," Beatrix says at the end of the tale, "I prefer to live in the country, like Timmy Willie."

WILLIAM HEELIS'S GOLF CLUBS

COUNTRY LIFE

BEATRIX POTTER HAD ALWAYS preferred the country to the town. Her American visitors shared her nostalgia for a rural but changing world. "They appreciate the memories of old times, the simple country pleasures – the homely beauty of the old farm house, the sublime beauty of the silent lonely hills." All her life, in her tales and elsewhere, she recorded "memories of old times" in loving detail.

TIMMY WILLIE, A COUNTRY MOUSE, IN RESIN

Old Mrs. Rabbit earns a living by selling rabbit-wool mittens, rosemary tea, and lavender rabbit-tobacco.

COTTAGE INDUSTRY

Beatrix knew farming was hard, but few of her tales look beyond the farmhouse and barnyard to the realities of toiling in the fields and hills. Even so, her characters are always busy. They raise children, do housework, and support themselves by taking in laundry, selling produce, or working as gardeners, cooks, gamekeepers (and poachers).

Ribby sits before the fire in The Tale of the Pie and the Patty-Pan. *The kitchen stove was the heart of every farmhouse – for cooking, boiling a kettle, drying the laundry, or sitting and chatting.*

COUNTRY NOTES

"It sometimes happens that a town child is more alive to the fresh beauty of the country than a child who is country born. My brother and I were born in London... But our descent – our interest and our joy were in the north country."

1942, LOOKING BACK

LONDON, 1880s – FROM FLEET STREET TO ST. PAUL'S

"I was very sorry to come away ... I think one of my pleasantest memories of Esthwaite is sitting on Oatmeal Crag ... with all the little tiny fungus people singing and bobbing and dancing in the grass and under the leaves all down below ... and I sitting up above and knowing something about them."

1896, AT THE END OF A VACATION IN THE LAKE DISTRICT

VILLAGE SUPPLIES

Countryfolk were more self-sufficient than we are today, but they still relied on a well-stocked village shop for the day-to-day essentials they couldn't grow or make at home. Sugar, snuff, and shiny galoshes are available at Ginger & Pickles', tea, marmalade and gossip at Tabitha Twitchit's. And tradesmen travel out to the countryside selling fresh produce from the local grocer, fishmonger, butcher, and baker.

TIMOTHY ASKEW AND HIS BAKER'S CART IN *THE TALE OF GINGER AND PICKLES*

The village policeman looks out for stray or unlicensed animals like Pickles and (above) Pigling Bland's brother.

The Windermere ferry carried people, horses, and goods across the lake on their way to and from local market towns such as Hawkshead.

GOING TO MARKET

Town and country are never far apart, even in Beatrix Potter's world. Farmers drive to market to sell their livestock and go shopping. Or they hire carriers to deliver their produce. (It's a carrier who delivers a hamper of vegetables and Timmy Willie to town.) Instead of tractors and cars, they travel by horses and carts. So every village has a forge, where a blacksmith shoes the horses and mends the carts.

OFF TO MARKET IN *THE TALE OF LITTLE PIG ROBINSON*

"…a succession of motor cars going along the valley below; it is our first experience of the nasty beasts in the country. There is no polite word for them & how they do s***k!"

1905, ON VACATION IN WALES

"There is a beastly fly-swimming spluttering aeroplane careering up & down over Windermere; it makes a noise like 10 million bluebottles."

1911, LIVING IN THE LAKE DISTRICT

"'Beatrix Potter' has very much at heart an appeal to raise a fund to save a strip of foreshore woodland and meadow, near Windermere Ferry, from imminent risk of disfigurement by extensive building and town extension. So many nice kind Americans come through the Lake district on their tour, some of them ask after Peter Rabbit. Do you think any of them would give a guinea [about $5] to help this fund, in return for an autographed drawing?"

1927, CAMPAIGNING FOR THE COUNTRYSIDE

"I was displeased one hot summer to see people going from cars to the lake. It is so difficult with rules. The Miss Scotts took a gramophone to walse on the ice; a general habit of gramophoning and wirelessing would be a great nuisance."

1940, ON THE IMPACT OF TOURISM

JOHNNY TOWN-MOUSE BRONZE FIGURINE C. 1913

THE FAIRY CARAVAN

"IN THE LAND OF Green Ginger there is a town called Marmalade, which is inhabited exclusively by guinea-pigs." A guinea pig called Tuppenny runs away and joins Alexander and William's Circus, which travels in a caravan. Beatrix first wrote down the tale of Tuppenny in 1903. In 1929, one of her American visitors, Alexander McKay of Philadelphia, persuaded her to produce another book, starting with Tuppenny, which he would publish especially for her American public.

Crowds of short-haired guinea pigs swarm around Messrs. Ratton & Scratch to buy hair elixir made of Arabian moonshine. Abyssinian Cavies are affronted.

FROM GULLIVER TO TUPPENNY

Satirist Jonathan Swift (1667–1745) set *Gulliver's Travels* in a fantasy world but used the story to poke fun at the snobbery of English society. Beatrix did the same with the town of Marmalade. Abyssinian Cavies have long hair and side whiskers. They look down on the common short-haired guinea pigs and find their twitterings tiresome.

The picture of Tuppenny being given a bottle of moonshine is based on one of five pictures Beatrix drew for an earlier story about a guinea pig being treated for a toothache.

SHORT-HAIRED GUINEA PIG

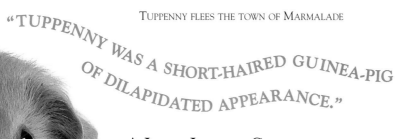

TUPPENNY FLEES THE TOWN OF MARMALADE

"TUPPENNY WAS A SHORT-HAIRED GUINEA-PIG OF DILAPIDATED APPEARANCE."

A LONG LINE OF GUINEA PIGS

In 1893, before Beatrix had guinea pigs of her own, she borrowed some to draw for a card. One had a long white ruff, and was named after Elizabeth I. "This PIG – offspring of *Titwillow the Second*, descendant of the *Sultan of Zanzibar*, and distantly related to a still more illustrious animal named the *Light of Asia* – this wretched pig took to eating blotting paper, pasteboard, string and other curious substances, and expired in the night."

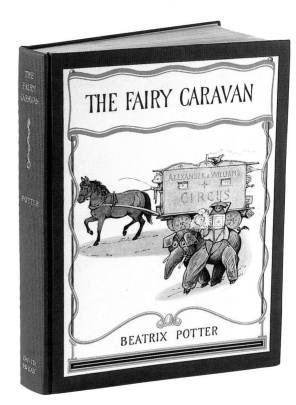

Warne was upset that Beatrix chose another publisher for the first edition of The Fairy Caravan *(above).*

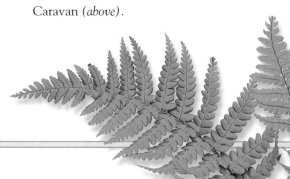

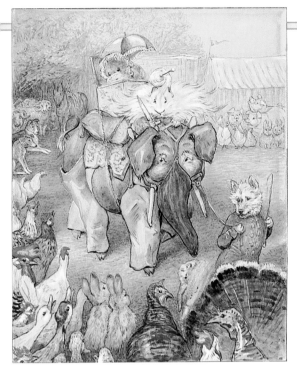

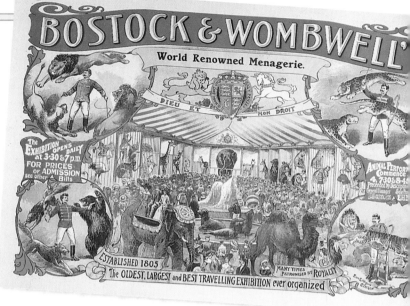

Tuppenny's new hair is ridiculed in Marmalade but the circus company admires it prodigiously. They dress him up as the Sultan of Zanzibar, and put him on The Pygmy Elephant with Princess Xarifa. At gala performances, his whiskers are dyed pink.

Traveling circuses put up posters to announce their arrival. Tuppenny's circus advertised "The Pygmy Elephant! The Learned Pig! The Fat Dormouse of Salisbury! Live Polecats and Weasels!"

BEATRIX GOES TO THE CIRCUS

Traveling circuses were universally popular in Beatrix Potter's day. In 1895, she described the one she saw while on vacation in the Lake District, to Eric Moore. "Half the school children in Ambleside were there, and several little boys tried to ride but the ponies went down on their knees & tumbled them off right & left."

MR. GINNET'S CIRCUS BULL, FROM A LETTER TO ERIC MOORE IN 1895

INVISIBLE ADVENTURES

As Tuppenny and his friends travel through the countryside around Sawrey, they meet Beatrix Potter's farm animals and swop stories. Fern seed makes them invisible to humans. At the end, they move on. But as Beatrix knew, circuses always return. "I can trace my pony's fairy footsteps, and hear his eager neighing. I can hear the rattle of the tilt-cart's wheels, and the music of the Fairy Caravan."

Beatrix dedicated The Fairy Caravan to Henry P. Coolidge (right), who had visited her from the United States in 1927.

HENRY P.

When thirteen-year-old Henry P. Coolidge came to meet Beatrix with his parents, she showed him her guinea pig story. They became firm friends. "I can quite believe that when Henry P was a very very small white headed baby he may have been acquainted with fairies, like I was, if there are fairies in New England." Her pet guinea pig (also called Tuppenny) had just died. So Henry P. sent her two new ones from Harrods store in London – Mrs. Tuppenny and Henry P.

FERNS

ABYSSINIAN CAVIE

"MY! WHAT A MOP OF HAIR; IT'S FULL OF HAY SEEDS."

FAIRY FEET & FLEECY FLOCKS

THE LIFELIKE PORTRAITS OF friendly sheep, sheep dogs, and other farm animals in *The Fairy Caravan* (and of Mrs. Fleecy Flock in *The Tale of Little Pig Robinson*) were set in hills and fields belonging to Beatrix Potter and her neighbors. Beatrix now had several farms. One was at Troutbeck, to the north of Sawrey. In the lonely hills above Troutbeck, she once saw four wild ponies cantering around a tree. Their tracks gave her the idea of a fairy caravan.

PONY BILLY LEAVES FAIRY FOOTSTEPS IN *THE FAIRY CARAVAN*

HERDWICK SHEEP AT THE TOP OF TROUTBECK, IN *THE FAIRY CARAVAN*

SUCH A LONELY PLACE

In 1940, a young American friend, Nancy Dean, wanted some news about the Fairy Caravan. Beatrix wrote back. "Where can the circus have wandered to? I believe I know! Right away amongst the fells – the green & blue hills above my sheep farm in Troutbeck. Such a lonely place, miles along a lovely green road. That was where I first saw the mark of little horse shoes."

Beatrix bought Troutbeck Park Farm (left) in 1924. She already owned three farms in Sawrey, but this 2,000-acre (800 hectares) sheep farm was her biggest purchase so far.

(RIGHT) CLOSE-UP OF HERDWICK SHEEP

A BREED APART

At Troutbeck, Beatrix and her shepherd Tom Storey built up a large herd of over 1,000 Herdwick sheep, a hardy local breed that has grazed in the fells for thousands of years. Herdwick are hefted – flocks know their patch and won't stray from it. As the lambs in *The Fairy Caravan* sing, "let us alone and we'll come home, and bring our tails behind us!"

HERDWICK RAM, WITH THE HEFTING INSTINCT IN HIS GENES

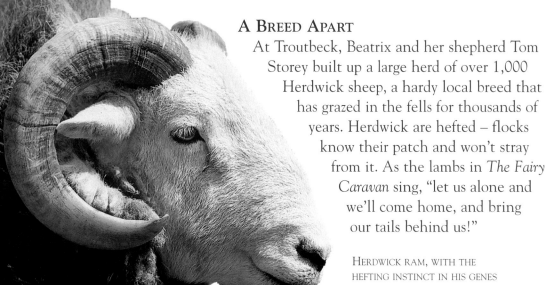

Beatrix sketched some of her favorite dogs in 1929, for copies of The Fairy Caravan *that were printed for local friends.*

SHEEP DOGS TO THE RESCUE

"Dizziness is unknown to Herdwick sheep," as an old ewe tells the Fairy Caravan. But stuck in a snowdrift high on a crag, even a level-headed Herdwick relies on being rescued by dogs scratching and shepherds prodding the drift with the long handles of their crooks.

MEG, FLY, AND OTHER SHEEP DOGS JOIN IN THE NIGHT-TIME SONGS AND STORIES AT THE SMITHY IN *THE FAIRY CARAVAN*

Beatrix poses with a judge, shepherds, and prize-winning Herdwick sheep at Keswick show (left).

BEATRIX AT KESWICK SHOW, 1935 (RIGHT)

CHAMPION CUP AWARDED TO BEATRIX FOR BEST HERDWICK EWE

EXACTING CRITICS

Beatrix hoped *The Fairy Caravan* would please "my most exacting critics – my own shepherds and blacksmith. I do not care tuppence about anybody else's opinion." They did like it, "only they are all claiming bits, and disputing who's who." For faraway readers like young Henry P. Coolidge, she wrote "explains" about the local settings, names, and old words in the book.

KEEP THE TARRIE WOO'

In 1930, Beatrix became President of the Herdwick Sheepbreeders' Association, and for the rest of her life promoted their cause. So does *The Fairy Caravan*: "pass the lineage forward; keep the tarrie woo' unsoftened! [The coarse wool was daubed with the owner's mark in tar.] Hold the proud ancient heritage of our Herdwick sheep."

LITTLE PIG ROBINSON

"WHEN I WAS A CHILD I used to go to the seaside for the holidays." So begins the last of the Peter Rabbit books. At a little town where there was a harbor and fishing boats and fishermen, a white cat called Susan is surprised to see a pig on board a ship. But Beatrix knew all about him. She first told his story in 1894, in a letter from the same little seaside town. In 1930, she finished *The Tale of Little Pig Robinson*, for Alexander McKay in Philadelphia and Warne in London.

SUSAN SEES LITTLE PIG ROBINSON ON BOARD *THE POUND OF CANDLES*

BEATRIX POTTER'S SKETCH OF ROWING BOATS AT TEIGNMOUTH

A picture of Little Pig Robinson being given a bath by his aunts at Piggery Porcombe appeared in the American edition only.

A VACATION LETTER

In 1894, while Beatrix was on vacation in Falmouth, a fishing port in Devon, she sent a picture letter to Eric Moore. "I was looking at a ship called *The Pearl of Falmouth* ... when I heard something grunt!" It was a pig, with no name, who rowed away to Robinson Crusoe's island and grew fat.

SEASIDE LOCATIONS

In 1941, Beatrix was asked where the tale was set. "'Stymouth' was Sidmouth on the south coast of Devonshire... the steep street looking down hill into the sea, and some of the thatched cottages were near Lyme... Ilfracombe gave me the idea of the long flight of steps down to the harbour… The shipping – including a pig aboard ship, was sketched at Teignmouth, S. Devon. The tall wooden shed for drying nets is (or was?) a feature of Hastings, Sussex. So the illustrations are a comprehensive sample of our much battered coasts."

BEATRIX ABOARD A BOAT IN FALMOUTH, 1894

WOODEN STILE NEAR SIDMOUTH (ABOVE)

Aunt Dorcas and Aunt Porcas send Little Pig Robinson shopping, over the fields to Stymouth. They are too stout to squeeze through the stiles.

THIS LITTLE PIG WENT TO MARKET

Market day at Stymouth is full of sights and sounds Beatrix had recorded in her vacation letters and journals on the south coast: seagulls and steamboats, a cat looking for fish on the quays and a coal cart splashing into the water, a dog with a stumpy tail, a goat-drawn cart. In the confusion, Little Pig Robinson allows himself to be led away by a sailor to *The Pound of Candles*. If only he had known ... that man was a ship's cook!

STREET SCENE IN
LYME REGIS, 1904

To a country-bred pig like Little Pig Robinson, the noise in Stymouth is confusing and dreadful.

DR. DOLITTLE, I PRESUME?

In 1930, a friend sent a copy of Hugh Lofting's American classic, *The Voyages of Dr. Dolittle* (1922). Beatrix was amused. "I also have taken a voyage, in imagination; and sent my Pig Robinson to the southern seas; but I think my adventures are cribbed from *Robinson Crusoe*, 'per' Stevenson's *Kidnapped*. There is nothing new under the sun."

The ship's cat and Little Pig Robinson see a shoal of silvery fish. Half the crew goes fishing but the cook is looking forward to pork.

LITTLE PIG ROBINSON
JUMPS SHIP

"IT PLEASED HIM TO EAT A GREAT DEAL AND TO LIE ON THE WARM BOARDS OF THE DECK".

A HAPPY ENDING

Little Pig Robinson heard he was being fattened up for roast pork, and rowed off to the land of the Bong tree. Visitors such as the Owl and the Pussy Cat (from the Edward Lear poem from 1871) found him well. "He grew fatter and fatter and more fatterer; and the ship's cook never found him."

BEATRIX POTTER'S SKETCH FOR *THE OWL AND THE PUSSY-CAT*, 1897

THE LAST YEARS

"I AM 'WRITTEN OUT' for story books," Beatrix Potter told a friend in 1934, "and my eyes are too tired for painting; but I can still take pleasure in old oak – and drains – and old roofs – and damp walls – oh the repairs ... Such are the problems that occupy my declining years!" She was buying more farmhouses and farmland in the Lake District, and taking care of them – not only for her own enjoyment but also to ensure that the old way of life there could continue.

BEATRIX POTTER, PHOTOGRAPHED AT HILL TOP IN 1943

FROM BEATRIX POTTER'S LAST STORY, *THE CHINESE UMBRELLA*

MORE VISITORS

Each summer a group of Girl Scouts camped on Beatrix Potter's land in Sawrey. "It is surely a blessing when old age is coming to be able still to understand and share the joy of life that is being lived by the young." On her last birthday, they came to see her at Castle Cottage, dressed up as characters from the tales. "I had to give prizes lavishly."

Beatrix with a group of Girl Scout visitors to Sawrey c. 1940. "If I lived in a tent," she chuckled, "I might get sciatica."

INSCRIPTION FROM BEATRIX POTTER IN GIRL SCOUT JOAN THORNELY'S AUTOGRAPH BOOK, 1931

PEKINESE, ORIGINALLY FROM IMPERIAL CHINA

FOOTWARMERS

Beatrix continued to acquire new pets. "We have a queer little animal here, a small female Pekinese," she told an American friend in 1936. "The collies don't like her; she is impertinent." Soon there were two Pekes, Tzuzee and Chuleh. When Beatrix became ill in the winter of 1943, and had to stay indoors, she said, "the little dogs are great company – most efficient footwarmers."

Five-year-old Alison Hart came with her parents from Blackpool, England, in 1942 to visit Beatrix and her two Pekes at Castle Cottage.

A LAST STORY

For Christmas 1942, Beatrix sent her young friend Alison Hart a story called *The Chinese Umbrella*. It features an umbrella with a duck's head handle, which disappears. The umbrella belongs to Beatrix Potter's tenant at Hill Top, Louie Choyce (who also received a copy of the story). Beatrix suspects that her pekinese dog Chuleh is the culprit. "Pekes know all about umbrellas, because the first umbrellas came from China."

CHINESE FIGURINE AT HILL TOP (LEFT)

The Emperor of China had an umbrella like the one in Beatrix Potter's last story. She drew him with eight little Pekes carrying his train and her own two bringing up the rear.

CHOCOLATE WAS RATIONED IN WARTIME BRITAIN BUT NOT IN THE US

WARTIME HARDSHIPS

World War II (1939–1945) placed Britain in a state of siege. Beatrix missed her American visitors but was cheered by their packages of chocolate and other luxuries that were rationed. As bombs fell on the cities, evacuees were sent to farms like hers. "What with shortage of petrol [gasoline] and 'flu," Beatrix admitted, "farming is a bit of a problem. But keep smiling!"

William Heelis joined the Home Guard, which watched for enemy planes and landing craft.

HILLSIDE IN SNOW, 1909 – BEATRIX HAD HER ASHES BURIED IN A SIMILAR SETTING

A SECRET BURIAL

Recurring illness sent Beatrix to her bed. "Thank God I have the seeing eye, that is to say, as I lie in bed I can walk step by step over the fells and rough land seeing every stone and flower and patch of bog and cotton pass where my old legs will never take me again." She died, aged 77, on December 22, 1943. At her request, her shepherd Tom Storey buried her ashes at Hill Top – only he knew where.

BEATRIX POTTER'S LEGACY

BEATRIX POTTER WORKED WITH the National Trust, the organization dedicated to the preservation of areas of historic interest or natural beauty around the UK. She managed several Lake District farms on the Trust's behalf and even bought one large estate, Monk Coniston, jointly with the Trust to prevent it from being split up. By the time she died, she owned over 4,000 acres (1,600 hectares). She left it all to the National Trust so that it should remain unspoiled forever.

PLAQUE COMMEMORATING THE NATIONAL TRUST'S FIRST PURCHASE, AT DERWENTWATER

ACORNS AND LEAVES FROM THE MIGHTY OAK, A SYMBOL FOR THE NATIONAL TRUST

Townend (left) is a 17th-century farmhouse on Troutbeck Park Farm, which Beatrix bought in 1923, and it appears in The Fairy Caravan.

IN TRUST FOR THE NATION

Beatrix was introduced to conservation by Canon Rawnsley, a founder of the National Trust. Thanks to their vision, the Lake District is still protected from development and farmed in traditional ways that have shaped the landscape for centuries. As Beatrix said, "It seems that we have done a big thing."

YEW TREE FARM (ABOVE), WITH A
COVERED GALLERY FOR SPINNING WOOL

YEW TREES AND A SHARD FENCE
(ABOVE) AT HIGH YEWDALE FARM

TARN HOWS (BELOW), ON THE
MONK CONISTON ESTATE

LOW TILBERTHWAITE (ABOVE) – LIKE HIGH
YEWDALE AND YEW TREE FARMS, PART OF
THE MONK CONISTON ESTATE

"In the calm spacious days that seem so long ago, I loved to wander on Troutbeck Fell. Sometimes I had with me an old sheep dog, 'Nip' or 'Fly'; more often I went alone. But never lonely. There was company of gentle sheep, and wild flowers and singing waters."

LONG LIVE PETER RABBIT!

MILLIONS OF PEOPLE HAVE MET Peter Rabbit. He began by losing his coat in Mr. McGregor's garden. Now he is the international star of books, ballet, and film, with his own website too. Who knows where this naughty rabbit will pop up next?

FOLLOW THAT RABBIT!

BEATRIX POTTER WAS AMAZED and amused by the fame of her naughty rabbit. Why is he so popular? Maurice Sendak, the great American author and illustrator of children's books, loves him as "both endearing little boy and expertly drawn rabbit." This timeline tracks Peter's meteoric rise.

1893:
Beatrix Potter first tells the story of Peter Rabbit, in a picture letter to five-year-old Noel Moore.

1902:
Frederick Warne & Co. publish *The Tale of Peter Rabbit* – the story has been in print ever since.

1904:
The Tale of Peter Rabbit is first published in the United States by Henry Altemus & Co., in an unauthorized pirate edition.

1904:
Peter Rabbit gets his coat back, in *The Tale of Benjamin Bunny.*

1904:
The first Peter Rabbit dolls go on sale (right), made by Steiff of Germany.

1909:
Peter Rabbit pops up again, in *The Tale of the Flopsy Bunnies* and *The Tale of Ginger and Pickles.*

1912:
Peter Rabbit learns how to paint, in *Peter Rabbit's Painting Book.*

1912:
The Tale of Peter Rabbit is published in Dutch, as *Het Verhaal van Pieter Langoor* (now *Pieter Konijn*).

1921:
The Tale of Peter Rabbit is printed in Braille.

1929:
The last book by Beatrix Potter to feature our hero is *Peter Rabbit's Almanac* (above).

1933:
Acclaimed British novelist Graham Green compares the "epic personalities" of Peter Rabbit and Benjamin Bunny to another famous duo, Don Quixote and Sancho Panza.

1917:
Peter Rabbit handkerchiefs and slippers (above) go on sale.

1912:
Peter Rabbit helps Benjamin Bunny rescue the Flopsy Bunnies in *The Tale of Mr Tod.*

1939–1945
World War II: *The Tale of Peter Rabbit* remains in print, despite paper shortages.

1936:
Walt Disney wants to film the Peter Rabbit books – Beatrix Potter declines.

1935:
Peter Rabbit learns some new songs, in two *Peter Rabbit Music Books.*

1946:
Three years after Beatrix Potter's death, her house at Hill Top opens to the public. It now attracts 75,000 Peter Rabbit fans each year.

1948:
The first Peter Rabbit figurine goes on sale, made by Beswick Ltd. in the UK.

1950s:
The myxomatosis virus reduces the UK rabbit population from 100 million to one million, but *The Tale of Peter Rabbit* lives on.

1962:
For Latin scholars young and old, *The Tale of Peter Rabbit* is published in translation as *Fabula de Petro Cuniculo.*

1965:
US pop group Dee Jay and the Runaways have a national hit with *Peter Rabbit*, a song by Tim Smith, a meatpacker from South Dakota. They sell 400,000 copies of the record.

1971:
Peter Rabbit stars in the full-length feature film of Sir Frederick Ashton's new ballet, *Tales of Beatrix Potter.*

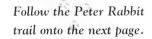

1965:
Hollywood star Vivien Leigh records Peter Rabbit nursery songs for EMI.

Follow the Peter Rabbit trail onto the next page.

ピーター ラビットの
おはなし

ビアトリクス・ポター さく・え
いしい ももこ やく

The Tale of Peter Rabbit
The Year of the Child

9p

世界一愛されたウサギ
The Best Loved Rabbit in the World
from the Land of Peter Rabbit

1971:
The Tale of Peter Rabbit is published in Japanese for the first time (above).

1979:
In the UK, Peter and friends feature on a stamp commemorating The Year of the Child.

1987:
Ladybird's simplified editions of the Peter Rabbit Books (retold and reillustrated with puppets) provoke a storm of protest in the UK.

1990:
A Peter Rabbit exhibition opens in Japan, and attracts 3,400 visitors a day, 120,000 visitors in total.

1992:
Peter Rabbit dances at Covent Garden, London, in the Royal Ballet's first staging of *Tales of Beatrix Potter.*

1991:
Fans flock to meet Peter Rabbit face to face in the new World of Beatrix Potter Attraction in the Lake District.

1992:
Peter Rabbit stars in the award-winning animation film, *The Tale of Peter Rabbit and Benjamin Bunny* (left), now showing on TV and video in over 50 countries.

1993:
Peter Rabbit is New York's Easter Bunny, appearing in Central Park and at the famous toy store FAO Schwarz.

1993:
A new Peter Rabbit stamp (above) is one of 10 celebrating favorite characters from British literature for children.

1993:
Peter Rabbit gets his own watch for his 100th birthday.

1993:
Peter Rabbit exhibitions tour the US, Australia, France, Scotland and London.

1993:
The Tales of Peter Rabbit, a mischievous musical is staged in New Zealand and Australia, to glowing reviews – "more bounce than a litter of frollicking baby bunnies" (*Sunday Herald Sun*).

1993:
A Peter Rabbit coin is issued in Gibraltar.

1996:
In New York, a Peter Rabbit balloon 20 feet (six metres) tall takes part in Macy's Thanksgiving Day Parade.

1996:
A US musical called *The Adventures of Peter Rabbit* goes on tour.

1996:
Publishers' Weekly magazine ranks *The Tale of Peter Rabbit* as America's best-selling children's classic of the century, after Janette Sebring Lowrey's *Pokey Little Puppy*.

1997:
Peter Rabbit pops up in a bookstore puppet show in the UK.

1997:
Peter Rabbit goes online at his award-winning multilingual website, www.peterrabbit.com.

1998:
Peter Rabbit gets his skates on for a Beatrix Potter ice spectacular at a popular UK theme park.

THE TALE OF
PETER RABBIT

BEATRIX POTTER
The original and authorized edition

1999:
Mr. McGregor's garden wins a gold medal at the world-famous Chelsea Flower Show in London. Visitors keep an eye out for Peter.

2000:
Peter Rabbit attends the White House Easter Egg Roll in Washington D.C.

2002:
The Tale of Peter Rabbit is 100 years old, and celebrates with a brand-new centenary edition.

PETER RABBIT GOES GLOBAL

THE TALE OF PETER RABBIT has come a long way since the first edition of 1902. In 1912 the first foreign translation was printed, *Het Verhaal van Pieter Langoor*, for Dutch readers. That was followed in 1921 by a translation into French, *l'Histoire de Pierre Lapin*, and, in time, more than 30 other languages.

WWW.PETERRABBIT.COM

In 1997, Peter launched his website. It was soon running in four languages, with more on the way and two million visitors a month. Animated adaptations of Beatrix Potter illustrations and a charming soundtrack bring the tales to life on screen. The website has won a host of awards for being packed with interesting facts, user-friendly, and safe for children.

WWW.PIERRELAPIN.COM.FR

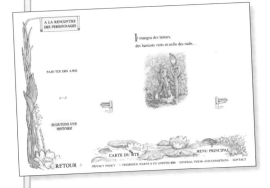

Peter Rabbit's website includes storytelling, facts about Beatrix Potter, interactive games and e-cards, news of events, and online shops for books and gifts.

WWW.PETERHASE.DE

WWW.PETERRABBIT.CO.JP

KOREAN EDITION OF *THE TALE OF PETER RABBIT*

EL CUENTO DE PEDRO EL CONEJO TRAVIESO

BEATRIX POTTER
LA EDICIÓN ORIGINAL Y AUTORIZADA

EDITORIAL SUDAMERICANA

SPANISH EDITION OF *THE TALE OF PETER RABBIT*, FOR SOUTH AMERICA

Het verhaal van **Pieter Konijn**

door Beatrix Potter

Ploegsma

DUTCH EDITION OF *THE TALE OF PETER RABBIT*

FRENCH EDITION
OF *PETER RABBIT*

Pierre Lapin

LA BIBLIOTHÈQUE DE PIERRE LAPIN
BEATRIX POTTER
Gallimard

ピーターラビットの
おはなし

ビアトリクス・ポター さく・え いしい ももこ やく

JAPANESE EDITION OF
THE TALE OF PETER RABBIT

B-215   小動物用
THE WORLD OF
PETER RABBIT™
RABBIT FOOD
ラビットフード 小粒

'NOW, my dears,' said old
Mrs. Rabbit one morning,
'you may go into the fields or down
the lane, but don't go into
Mr. McGregor's garden: your Father
had an accident there; he was put
in a pie by Mrs. McGregor.'

○満足成分配合○

Net wt. 600g

PET FOOD FOR RABBITS
(ABOVE) AND CHEWS TO
GNAW ON (ABOVE RIGHT)

THE WORLD OF
PETER RABBIT™

THE ULTIMATE FANS?

The Tale of Peter Rabbit was first
translated into Japanese in 1971.
Since then, Peter has gathered a huge
following in Japan. Over 1,300,000
copies of his book have been sold.
His image appears on everything from
refrigerator magnets to bathroom
scales, and flower pots to pet food.
Thousands of Japanese visitors flock
to Britain to trace Beatrix Potter's life
and see Peter Rabbit's world for
themselves. "Peter Rabbit dai-suki!" –
"I love you, Peter Rabbit!"

JAPANESE
TEA SET

*The Palace Hotel in Tokyo has a Peter Rabbit menu and a
Peter Rabbit suite that is decorated from top to bottom with
Peter Rabbit wallpaper, bedding, cushions, rugs, lamps,
pictures, and toys. Sweet dreams, everyone!*

PETER RABBIT GOES DANCING

IN 1971, FIVE TALES were turned into a ballet and filmed as *Tales of Beatrix Potter*, starring Squirrel Nutkin, Mr. Jeremy Fisher, Two Bad Mice, Jemima Puddle-duck, and Pigling Bland. Peter and others also joined in. In spectacular costumes and sets, dancers of Britain's Royal Ballet leaped and twirled to the music, bringing all the original magic to life. After the first screening, a tearful four-year-old said, "I didn't want it to end!"

JEMIMA PUDDLE-DUCK, STEPPING OUT WITH THE FOXY GENTLEMAN

SIR FREDERICK ASHTON, CHOREOGRAPHER OF *TALES OF BEATRIX POTTER*

FROM BOOK TO SCREEN
The film's designer and producer, Christine Edzard and Richard Goodwin, first wove the tales into a new story, then made costumes and sets true to Beatrix Potter's illustrations. The score used songs and dances from her childhood. Dancers rehearsed steps that showed off her animals' movement and character. Then the ballet was filmed, in a studio and on location in her Lake District.

SQUIRRELS WITH GIFTS (BELOW)   ON STAGE AT COVENT GARDEN, LONDON (ABOVE)

JOHNNY TOWN-MOUSE AND MRS. TITTLEMOUSE ON THEIR WAY TO THE GRAND FINALE, A PICNIC

Instead of tutus and tights, costumes had to match Beatrix Potter's illustrations and be made from lifelike materials – and yet be light enough to let this dancer move like a naughty rabbit!

TWO BAD MICE
IN A DANCER-SIZED
DOLLS' HOUSE

FEET TOGETHER
IN AN *ASSEMBLÉ*, A
GRACEFULLY FROGGY,
SIDEWAYS LEAP BY
MR. JEREMY FISHER

MRS. TIGGY-WINKLE,
ORIGINALLY DANCED
BY SIR FREDERICK
ASHTON

PIGLING BLAND AND PIG-WIG'S
PAS DE DEUX, A DANCE FOR TWO

FROM FILM TO STAGE

For the film, some scenes
were shot on large studio
sets that recreated Beatrix
Potter's miniatures on a
human, dancer's scale. Others
were shot outdoors, on location
in the Lake District. In 1992, the
Royal Ballet adapted *Tales of Beatrix
Potter* for the stage and performed it
at Covent Garden in London. The
ballet is very demanding for dancers
but a sheer delight for fans of
ballet or Beatrix or both.

PETER RABBIT ON SCREEN

WHEN MICKEY MOUSE took the world by storm in 1929, Walt Disney began looking for new characters for his films and thought of Peter Rabbit. Beatrix Potter was doubtful. "My drawings are not good enough," she wrote to her publisher. "To make Silly Symphonies they will have to enlarge them and that will show up all the imperfections." Sixty years later, Warne thought it might be possible after all.

OLD AND NEW
Everyone remembers Beatrix Potter's illustration of naughty Peter Rabbit jumping into Mr. McGregor's watering can to hide. Animation also shows what happens next, inside the can. It's cold, dark, and wet, and Peter is trying not to sneeze. A sound track adds music, sound effects, and voices.

THE SETTING
For each new scene, when the action is shown from one angle, an artist paints a new background. Mr. Jeremy Fisher's lake looks like the perfect spot to go fishing!

WHEEE! Peter and Benjamin swing on Mr. McGregor's scarecrow. Children in the Lake District supplied their voices.

THE STAR
Mr. Jeremy Fisher and his lily pad are on a separate, transparent sheet of celluloid or cel. Bold colors and a sharp outline make him the main focus. To bring him to life, new cels show every stage of every move.

ACTION!
It takes about 24 frames per second (each frame is one cel and background) to catch a fish, and a new background each time the angle or scene changes.

A BITE!

MR. JEREMY FISHER LANDS A STICKLEBACK

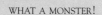
WHAT A MONSTER!

ARTIST AT WORK

Most animators work on computer now, but the tales were hand painted to capture the spirit of Beatrix Potter's original watercolors.

ANIMATOR AT HIS DRAWING BOARD

Benjamin and Peter were animated by Grand Slamm Partnership for TV Cartoons Ltd., which produced nine films in The World of Peter Rabbit and Friends™ *series, released between 1992 and 1996.*

COLORING IN

Beatrix Potter painted about 30 illustrations for each of her books. But it took a team of artists to produce about 32,000 frames for each film. To make sure their work was identical, color models specified the exact shades to be used for each character.

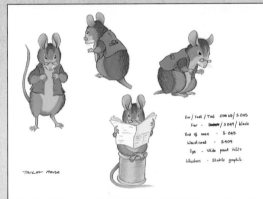

A PERFECT PICKLE

Artists also produced character models, close-ups from several angles to work out the shape, expression, and way of moving that give each animal its own unique look.

ALSO STARRING...

The films feature 14 of the best-known tales. Peter Rabbit and Benjamin Bunny star in the first film – here are the others.

MRS. TIGGY-WINKLE AND MR. JEREMY FISHER

VOICED BY
PRUNELLA SCALES
AND DEREK JACOBI

TOM KITTEN AND JEMIMA PUDDLE-DUCK

A LAKE DISTRICT CHILD
AND SU POLLARD

THE TAILOR OF GLOUCESTER

IAN HOLM

TWO BAD MICE AND JOHNNY TOWN-MOUSE

FELICITY KENDAL
AND RIK MAYALL,
AND HUGH LAURIE

PIGLING BLAND

CHRIS LANG

THE FLOPSY BUNNIES AND MRS. TITTLEMOUSE

LAKE DISTRICT CHILDREN
AND ANNA MASSEY

SAMUEL WHISKERS

STRUAN ROGER

MR. TOD

DINSDALE LANDEN

BEATRIX POTTER WAS
PLAYED BY
NIAMH CUSACK

PETER RABBIT FOREVER

ALL HER LIFE, Beatrix Potter hoarded and labeled everything she felt to be of significance – her secret journals, family photographs, sketchbooks, letters from friends, fans, and publishers, even the old marbles she found at Hill Top. Other people in turn treasured drawings, letters, and gifts from Beatrix. Since her death in 1943, the National Trust, the Frederick Warne Archive, private collectors, and public museums around the world have looked after this amazing legacy.

LESLIE LINDER (1904–1974), BRITISH ENGINEER TURNED BEATRIX POTTER COLLECTOR

IN SEARCH OF PETER RABBIT

Leslie Linder was the first to collect Beatrix Potter materials on a large scale. For 30 years he visited the Lake District, interviewed people she had known, and bought items at auction. He exhibited the best items in 1966, and produced two major studies of her work, *A History of the Writings of Beatrix Potter* and *The Art of Beatrix Potter*. His collections are now stored by the Victoria and Albert Museum, London, which has the world's largest archive of Beatrix Potter's art. Fans can see a small but regularly updated selection there.

VICTORIA AND ALBERT MUSEUM, LONDON

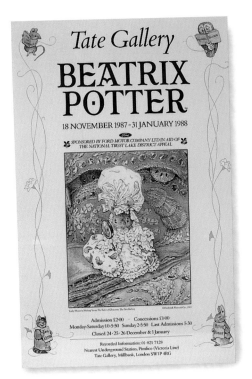

London's Tate Gallery houses the Tailor of Gloucester *illustrations. The Tate held a major exhibition of Beatrix Potter's work in 1987–1988, which attracted huge crowds.*

SPREADING THE WORD

Many of the people who continue to preserve her legacy belong to The Beatrix Potter Society. Set up in 1980, it promotes the study and appreciation of her life and work as an author, artist, diarist, farmer, and conservationist. It does this through lectures, visits, conferences, reports, and newsletters for over 800 members around the world.

CRACKING THE CODE

In 1952, Beatrix Potter's secret journals were discovered at Castle Cottage in Sawrey – seven volumes of over 200,000 words, which Beatrix wrote out in her own code from 1881 to 1897. Leslie Linder cracked the code in 1958, and Warne published his translation in 1966, the centenary of her birth. It is a wonderful window into Beatrix Potter's world.

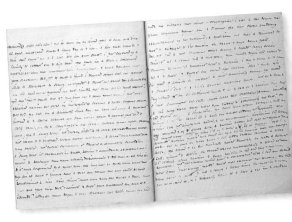

JOURNAL AT THE BEATRIX POTTER GALLERY IN HAWKSHEAD, CUMBRIA

THE BEATRIX POTTER SOCIETY'S MOUSE

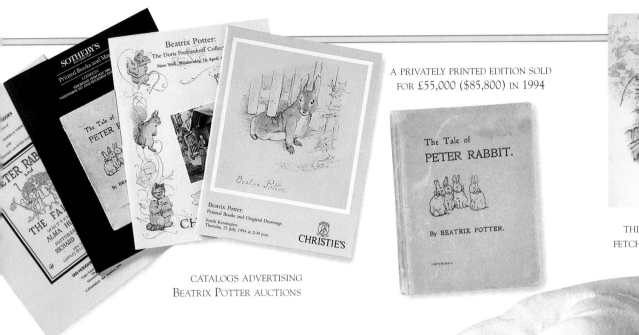

CATALOGS ADVERTISING
BEATRIX POTTER AUCTIONS

A PRIVATELY PRINTED EDITION SOLD
FOR £55,000 ($85,800) IN 1994

This Pig went to Market;
This Pig staid at home;

THIS PIG WENT TO MARKET – AND
FETCHED £65,000 ($107,250) IN 1999

LOOKING AFTER PETER RABBIT

Two curators look after more than 3,000 Beatrix Potter items in the Frederick Warne Archive. Their job is to add new and important items and to catalog, study, and conserve each one – for future generations to treasure.

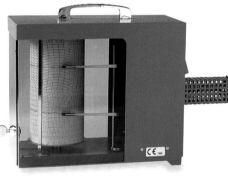

WARNE'S THERMOHYGROGRAPH, WHICH
MONITORS HUMIDITY AND TEMPERATURE

HANDLE WITH CARE

The Tale of Peter Rabbit water-colors are over 100 years old, fragile, and irreplaceable. They are mounted on acid-free board, sealed in frames, wrapped in dust-free, scratch-resistant cloth, and locked in a safe. For very special occasions, they are lent to museums for the public to enjoy.

Peter Rabbit *watercolors have blue covers, nicknamed pyjamas. Illustrations from Cicely Mary Barker's* Flower Fairies *(1923–) have pink covers, called nighties!*

A PETER RABBIT MAP

ALL OVER BRITAIN, Beatrix Potter fans can see the hills, woods and lakes, gardens and market towns that inspired her little books. Here are some of the places associated with key parts of her life and work. (The starred visitor attractions are open to the public.)

THE LAKE DISTRICT

DERWENTWATER, HOME TO SQUIRREL NUTKIN

ST. HERBERT'S ISLAND (OWL ISLAND)

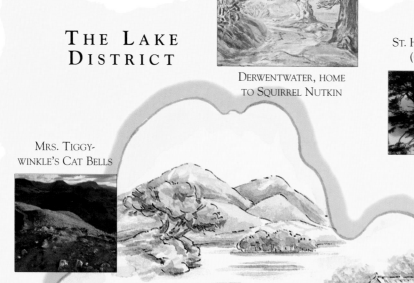

MRS. TIGGY-WINKLE'S CAT BELLS

★ BEATRIX POTTER EXHIBITION

THE LAKE DISTRICT

The National Trust guides visitors through Beatrix Potter's beloved farmhouse and garden in Sawrey. In nearby Hawkshead, original illustrations and other treasures are on display in the Beatrix Potter Gallery.

GWAENY THE FL BUNNIES' G

DERWENTWATER

★ BEATRIX POTTER GALLERY

TROUTBECK

SETTING FOR *THE FAIRY CARAVAN*

HAWKSHEAD

BOWNESS

SAWREY

MR. McGREGOR'S POND

GLOUCESTER

Number 9 College Court, where Beatrix Potter set the Tailor of Gloucester's house, is now a Peter Rabbit giftshop. On show are superb replicas of the mayor's new clothes – and the tailor's mice!

PIGLING BLAND'S CROSSROADS

★ HILL TOP, BEATRIX POTTER'S HOUSE

JEMIMA AND KEP'S TOWER BANK ARMS

THE *PIE AND THE PATTY-PAN* GARDEN

★ WORLD OF BEATRIX POTTER ATTRACTION

MOSS ECCLES TARN, ONE OF MR. JEREMY FISHER'S LAKES

★ TAILOR OF GLOUCESTER SHOP

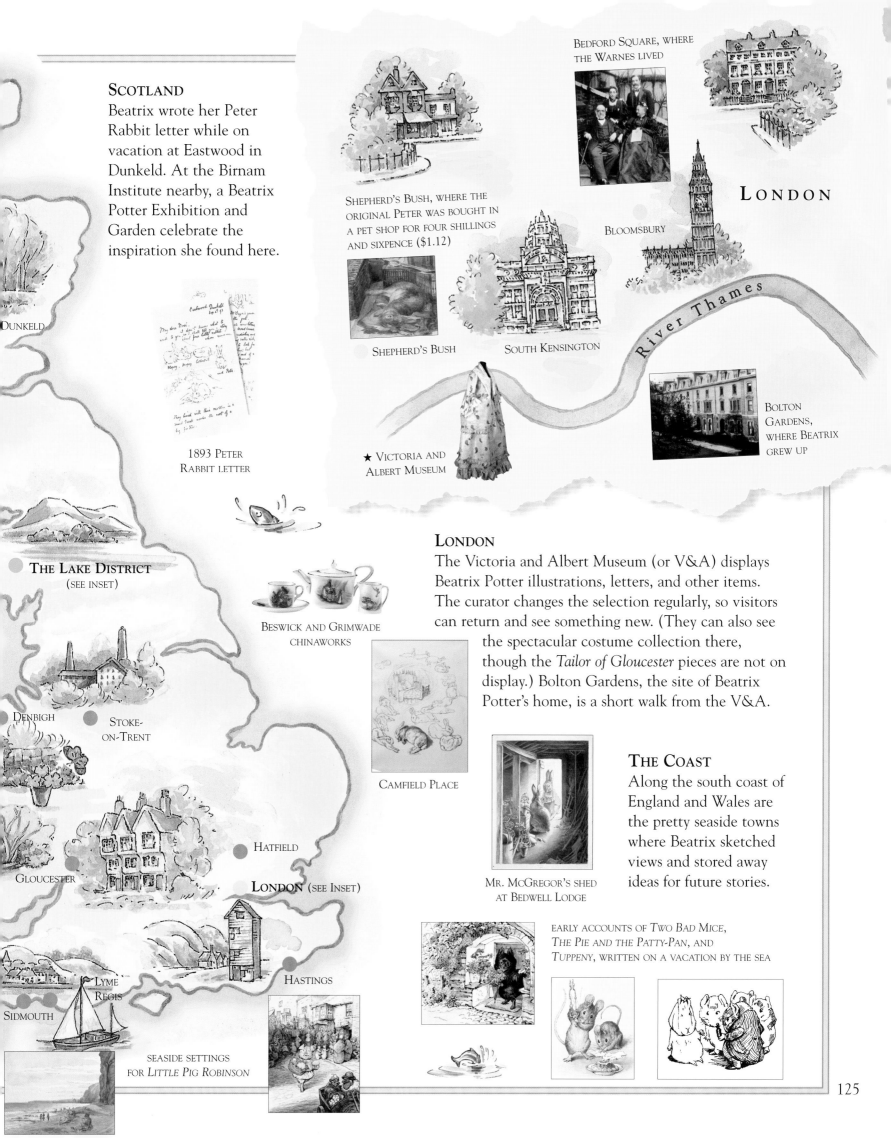

SCOTLAND

Beatrix wrote her Peter Rabbit letter while on vacation at Eastwood in Dunkeld. At the Birnam Institute nearby, a Beatrix Potter Exhibition and Garden celebrate the inspiration she found here.

DUNKELD

1893 PETER
RABBIT LETTER

THE LAKE DISTRICT
(SEE INSET)

BESWICK AND GRIMWADE
CHINAWORKS

DENBIGH

STOKE-
ON-TRENT

CAMFIELD PLACE

GLOUCESTER

HATFIELD

LONDON (SEE INSET)

LYME
REGIS

SIDMOUTH

HASTINGS

SEASIDE SETTINGS
FOR *LITTLE PIG ROBINSON*

BEDFORD SQUARE, WHERE
THE WARNES LIVED

LONDON

SHEPHERD'S BUSH, WHERE THE
ORIGINAL PETER WAS BOUGHT IN
A PET SHOP FOR FOUR SHILLINGS
AND SIXPENCE ($1.12)

BLOOMSBURY

SHEPHERD'S BUSH

SOUTH KENSINGTON

River Thames

BOLTON
GARDENS,
WHERE BEATRIX
GREW UP

★ VICTORIA AND
ALBERT MUSEUM

LONDON

The Victoria and Albert Museum (or V&A) displays Beatrix Potter illustrations, letters, and other items. The curator changes the selection regularly, so visitors can return and see something new. (They can also see the spectacular costume collection there, though the *Tailor of Gloucester* pieces are not on display.) Bolton Gardens, the site of Beatrix Potter's home, is a short walk from the V&A.

THE COAST

Along the south coast of England and Wales are the pretty seaside towns where Beatrix sketched views and stored away ideas for future stories.

MR. MCGREGOR'S SHED
AT BEDWELL LODGE

EARLY ACCOUNTS OF *TWO BAD MICE*,
THE PIE AND THE PATTY-PAN, AND
TUPPENY, WRITTEN ON A VACATION BY THE SEA

INDEX

ACKNOWLEDGMENTS

Dorling Kindersley would like to thank Frederick Warne & Co.
for illustrations taken from Beatrix Potter's books and for sketches,
photographs, letters, early editions, and other items
from the Frederick Warne Archive.

JEMIMA IN RESIN,
FROM THE FREDERICK
WARNE ARCHIVE

MINIATURE MAILBAG,
FROM THE FREDERICK
WARNE ARCHIVE

Dorling Kindersley would also like to thank:

Abbreviations key: a = above, b = below, c = center, l = left, r = right, t = top
AKG London: 15br (Sir John Tenniel, 1820–1914); Armitt Trust: 19bc; British Museum 48trb, 55br, 76tl, tr, cl, 77tc, 124cra; The Beatrix Potter Society: 12bc, 122br; Bridgeman Art Library, London/New York: 15tl (William Powell Frith, 1819–1909); Grimsthorpe Castle, Lincolnshire, UK 38bl (William Hogarth, 1697–1764); New Walk Museum, Leicester City Museum Service, UK 18–19tc (William Powell Frith, 1819–1909); John Noott Galleries, Broadway, Worcestershire, UK 62–63c (Richard Jack, 1866–1952); RSA, London, UK 12tr (by John Callcott Horsley, 1817–1903); Russell-Cotes Art Gallery and Museum, Bournemouth, UK 25br (Anna Lea Merritt, 1844–1930); Buckle Yeat: 60bl, 124bc; Dee Conway: 118bl; Bill Cooper: 110c, 118clb, bc, 118–119c, 119c; Corbis: 107clb; David Reed 118cla; Brian S. Turner/FLPA 42bl; Andy Crawford and Kit Houghton: 100tl; Mary Evans Picture Library: 99cl; Rare Book Department, The Free Library of Philadelphia: 38tc; Anthony Gaddum: 17clb; GAF Guenther Pfeiffer GmbH: 80bc, 128br; Ronald Grant Archive: 113ca; The Guide Association (UK): 106cl, cr; Robert Harding Picture Library: 116–117c; Harrods Limited, Company Archive: 33tl; The Horn Book Inc., 56 Roland Street, Suite 200, Boston MA 02129, 617-625-0225: 83cr, bc, br; MS Typ 789, Department of Printing and Graphics, Houghton Library of the Harvard College Library: 20tl, 42ca; Hulton Archive: 29cr, 30bl, 48tr, 49cl, 62bc, 63tc, 83tl, 98bc, 121tc; Sean Hunter: 12cl; Imperial War Museum: 89br; Lakes Story Ltd: 38–39c, 124br; Linder Trust: 13r, 14tl, br, 16c, 17cla, cr, 39cl, 46br, 48br, 52ca, 58tr, 64–65b, 69cr; 78c, 78–79tc, 80cl, 85br, 94tr, 95tc, 96tr, cr, 122tr, 125tc; London Zoo: 82tr; National Art Library, V&A: 71tr (Randolph Caldecott, 1846–1886); MS-Papers-0461, Alexander Turnbull Library, National Library of New Zealand: 30cl; National Trust: 4r, 5br, 6b, 12br, 14bl, 18c, 23br, 30tl, 31br, 36, 37tl, 41br, 42tl, tr, cb, 43cl, clb, cr, 44tr, 44–45c, 46tl, tc, bl, 47tr, c, 48bc, 50tl, tc, tcb, tr, c, cr, bl, bc, br, 51tl, tc, tr, trb, bl, 52tl, cb, 53b, 54c, b, 55t, 58tl, cl, 59cr, crb, bl, 60tr, cl, cr, 61cl, c, cb, bra, 62tr, 63tr, c, cr, bc, br, 64tl, 65c, tr, trb, 66tl, tr, cl, cr, 67tl, tr, cr, 68tl, cl, c, 69tl, bra, 70tl, cl, crb, bc, 71tl, tlb, cl, 72–74, 75tl, tr, trb, bl, cra, br, 77tr, 78tl, cl, cr, 78–79c, 79tc, bl, 80tr, c, crb, 81tl, 82tl, cl, cb, 83tr, 84tl, cl, c, r, 85tr, 86b, 87br, 88tr, bra, 88–89c, 89cr, 90tl, bl, 91tc, c, 92tl, bc, br, 93tc, 94tl, c, 95br, 96tl, cl, bc, 97tc, r, 98cl, clb, bl, bc, tr, 99tc, tr, cr, crb, bc, 101ca, 103cr, bc, 104tl, tr, ca, br, 105tl, c, crb, 107tc, 112c, clb, 113tl, 122cr, 124tcl, cl, crb, bl, 125bc, bcl, bcr, 126tr, cl, br, bl, 127tc, tr, br; National Trust Photographic Library: 45tr (Frederick Yates, 1854–1919); Matthew Antrobus 108cl; Val Corbett 44–45b; Joe Cornish 58c, 85cb, 102bl, 108tr, 108–109b, 109cl, c, 124cla; Rod. J. Edwards 90–91c; David Levenson 86t; Nadia MacKenzie 62br; Nick Meers 91crb; Stephen Robson 53cl, 109t; Robert Thrift: 102cl; Robert Opie Collection: 49tc, 83bl, 101tr, 107cla; the Palace Hotel in Tokyo: 117br; Cressida Pemberton-Pigott: 46c, 46–47c, 54t, 64–65t, 75crb, 124br; private collectors: 13bl, 16cr, 18tl, 19tr, cl, br, 23tr, 27bc, 28tl, cl, 30–31c, 31tr, 38cl, 40bl, 47br, 52tr, bl, 53tc, 59cl, 61tr, 79cb, 88cl, 89tc, tr, 92tr, 95cr, 97cl, 101cb, 103cl, 104bl, 106br, bc, 107tr, 124tr, 125tr; Royal Green Jackets Museum: 105ca; Major Tom Smith: 77cl; Leslie E. Spatt: 118tr, 119tc, cr, br; Tate Gallery: 37tr, 38tl, 39tr, bc, 40tl, c, 41tc, bc, 62ca; TDB 70bl, 81br; Tower Bank Arms: 69c, 124bc; TV Cartoons Limited: 11tr, 120–121 (not photo); Victoria and Albert Museum: 6t, 7, 8c, 8–9c, 12c, cb, 13t, cl, 14cl, c, 14–15c, 15cr, 16tr, bl, bc, 17tc, tr, bra, 18cr, 19c, bl, 20c, cl, 20–21bc, 21tr, c, cr, br, 22c, 23tl, 25cl, 28tr, bl, 29t, 39tc, c, cr, 40cl, r, br, 41l, 42br, 44tl, 47cr, 48cl, c, 51bra, 53tr, 59c, 62bl, 64cl, 65br, 66bl, 67tc, c, 68bl, 69tr, 71cr, cb, 76–77ba, 79tr, 82ca, cr, 84bl, 85ca, 88c, 90tr, 92–92c, 93tr, bl, 94bl, 95tl, 97cr, 102br, 104cl, cb, 105tr, br, 107br, 112ca, 125ca, cra, c, cb, bl, 126c, 127c; Barrie Watts: 50bla, 61bl; The World of Beatrix Potter Attraction: 111t, 124cb. Additional artwork: Alex Vining 56–57, 124–125. Jacket back photograph: National Trust Photographic Library: Val Corbett.

BEATRIX POTTER'S CLOGS, FROM
THE FREDERICK WARNE ARCHIVE

POLICEMAN DOLL,
FROM GAF
GUENTHER PFEIFFER
GmbH

THE TALE OF PIGLING BLAND

FIRST EDITION 1913,
FROM THE FREDERICK
WARNE ARCHIVE

Dorling Kindersley would also like to thank the following for their generous help:

The Copyrights Group Limited: Diana Neal, Jo Plumley, Linda Pooley, Theresa South;
The National Trust: Caroline Cotgrove, Charles Flanagan, Liz Hunter, Catherine Pritchard, Peter Tasker;
Peter Rabbit and Friends™, Covent Garden; Sotheby's: Catherine Porter;
Victoria and Albert Museum: Anne Hobbs, Susan North, Siobhan Summerfield;
and finally: Rose Horridge and Sarah Mills (picture research); Gary Hyde, Lisa Lanzarini and
Julia March (design support); Anna Trenter (proof-reading); Hilary Bird (index); everyone at Warne.

The author is indebted to the wealth of research by other writers, published by Warne:

Glen Cavaliero *Beatrix Potter's Journal*; Hunter Davies & Cressida Pemberton-Pigott *Beatrix Potter's Lakeland*; Rumer Godden *The Tale of Tales*; Anne Stevenson Hobbs *Beatrix Potter's Art*; Margaret Lane *The Tale of Beatrix Potter*; Leslie Linder *A History of the Writings of Beatrix Potter* and *The Journal of Beatrix Potter*; Jane Crowell Morse *Beatrix Potter's Americans* (published by Horn Book); Judy Taylor *Beatrix Potter's Letters*, *Letters to Children*, and (with Whalley, Stevenson Hobbs & Battrick) *Beatrix Potter 1866–1943*.

"It is much more satisfactory to address a real live child…" (Beatrix Potter, 1905)

The miniature letters featured in this book were written for the following children:
Lucie Carr 61; Andrew Fayle 30–31, 51, 59, 67; John Hough 76–77;
the Moore children 43, 63, 71, 80; John Ripley 30, 31, 47.